PROCESS AND PROGRESS PISTOL TRAINING

PROCESS AND PROGRESS PISTOL TRAINING

PROVEN METHODS TO STRUCTURE YOUR PRACTICE

DREW ESTELL

BAER
PUBLISHING

PROCESS AND PROGRESS PISTOL TRAINING
Proven Methods to Structure Your Practice

ISBN 978-1-5445-2243-2   *Paperback*
       978-1-5445-2242-5   *Ebook*

To all those who invested in me
so I could invest in others.

CONTENTS

INTRODUCTION

We've all had that moment on the range, during a competition match, or even in the shoot house. You see someone shooting fast splits, accurate shots, and their movements seem liquid, like second nature because they have the fundamentals down so well. It could even be on your computer screen as you watch a video of competitive shooter and firearms instructor Todd Jarrett doing a draw demonstration in front of a crowd.

I remember the first time I watched Todd do that demo. I thought to myself, "It took thirty years to get that good." The video starts off with Todd explaining his holster and how to defeat its retention or the mechanism holding the gun in place. After talking about the time it normally takes him to draw from his holster, he starts to demo a dry fire (shooting without ammunition), slowly at first, then progressively working up to faster draw times. He ends up drawing his gun and breaking the shot (aiming and firing) in 0.6 seconds. In another video, he does a "1R1" in 1.5 seconds. That's a One, Reload, One, in which he draws, shoots, reloads, and returns to the target for another shot in a second and a half. To draw and shoot one accurate shot in 1.5 seconds is a tough—but completely doable—goal for a lot of people. Todd, on the other hand, can move twice as fast and accomplish twice as much. How does he do it?

Hint: it has everything to do with training.

BETTER THAN WE WERE BEFORE

As I'm sure you have done, or are currently doing, I spent years listening to the advice of others and trying to make improvements in my training. The fact is, it didn't work, and I had to hold out for those aha moments where something clicked, and I finally understood what my instructors were trying to teach me. Unfortunately, most of the "instruction" I was given in my military and shooting career was only regurgitated information that those people, good people, were given when they were taught:

"Quit jerking the trigger!"

"You're anticipating the shot!"

"Slow down!"

"You're not using your sights!"

"Grip the gun harder!"

"Slow is smooth; smooth is fast!"

"Focus on the front sight, not the target!"

"Let the shot surprise you!"

I'm sure there is a host of other adages that you've heard from an instructor, your buddy on the range who's better than you, or the research you've done on the internet. It's not that most of these statements aren't true; it's that the person saying them doesn't understand their origin. Such statements speak more to the effects of, rather than the causes of, the problem. Someone who's not using their sights, for example, might not know how to do so correctly. Instead of just rightly proclaiming that I was "anticipating the shot," someone needed to explain to me how to stop anticipating the shot and, more importantly, what I should be doing instead.

Most instructors who make these empty statements mean well and may even be good shooters themselves. But being a good shooter doesn't make you a good coach. A successful instructor is someone who will lead you through drills each step of the way. A coach worth his or her salt will give you the what, the why, and the how to make sure you understand the reasoning behind each drill. It's knowing how your fundamentals build your mechanics—and how your mechanics build your abilities—that gives those statements meaning.

I can't promise that by the time you finish reading this book, you'll be one of the world's greatest shooters. Rather, the purpose of this book is to show you how I and others had to learn to think differently about shooting in order to diagnose problems with our technique, isolate deficiencies of skill, and put it all back together to become better than we were before.

INCREMENTAL IMPROVEMENTS

My shooting career started in the Army. Shortly after joining the Army, I completed training to become a Green Beret. I spent roughly ten years in Army Special Forces and completed a lot of training to improve my shooting. I never really improved, however, until I understood the intent of the different drills. Only once I grasped, conceptually, exactly what it was that I was trying to accomplish did my shooting evolve past anything other than mindlessly going through the motions.

The biggest key to my enlightenment was working with Dr. Seth Haselhuhn. A mental performance specialist, Seth helped me to develop the discipline necessary to achieve my goals. I reached out to him because I was tired, frustrated, and fed up with doing the same thing over and over again and expecting different results. This book is the product of that process, of the journey I undertook with Seth.

Each chapter of *Process and Progress* will introduce a new concept in shooting. Take the time to master one concept before moving onto the next. Doing so will dramatically shorten your learning curve—unless, that is, you like the idea of doing ten thousand reps. Then, by all means, keep doing whatever you were doing before.

I always thought I was a good shooter—until I didn't. If you are only meeting some external standard, then you aren't achieving your full potential. Even the best shooters in the world had to start somewhere. Do you think JJ Racaza, Ron Avery, or Kyle Lamb picked up a gun and shot a two-second bill drill on the first try? No, they didn't. It took years of work and purposeful practice for them to get to where they are. They didn't waste reps and say, "That's good enough." They recognized that mastery is a process, and they made incremental improvements on a daily, weekly, or monthly basis.

You can be a good shooter. You can also be a great shooter if you want. It doesn't matter who you are or where you came from. What matters is what you do and how you do it. The only thing that determines how fast you can put accurate rounds on target is your conscious decision to get better at doing it. Believe in yourself and know that you are in charge of your success and your failure. If no one has ever said that to you before, or you don't believe it, then read the following and finally realize that it's the truth:

You have everything it takes to be good at this.

You are ultimately responsible for your success and failure.

We all start somewhere. Where you're going is what matters.

A THIRTEEN-YEAR-OLD AMISH GIRL

One of the most humbling moments on my journey to becoming a better shooter came at a local United States Practical Shooting Association match. I was there with a couple of other Green Berets, whom I'll call Pax and Ryan. A young girl came to the match, and naturally, everyone there was open and willing to help make her first experience a good one. She showed up wearing an ankle-length denim skirt, a pair of running shoes, an athletic-style polo shirt, and a head cover. She was literally a thirteen-year-old Amish girl.

Me: Hi, I'm Drew. If you have any questions, let us know. We'd be happy to help you out.

Girl: Yes, sir, thank you very much.

Me: All right, well, have fun and let us know if you need anything.

She was up next, so she started to get her gear ready. I watched in astonishment as she pulled out an STI 2011 and put it in the holster.

Me: Huh, that's a really nice pistol.

Pax: Yeah, man, what the hell is she doing with that?

When it was the girl's turn, she walked up to the range officer running the stage. He asked her if she had any questions. She didn't. He reassured her that everything would be fine if she just took her time and watched her muzzle. "I'll be with you the whole time," he said.

What happened next is something I'll always remember.

"Shooter, do you understand the course of fire?" the ranger officer asked.

"Yes," the girl answered. Her demeanor had changed. We could clearly see that she was focused on what she was about to do. More focused than the rest of us usually were.

"Load and make ready."

With all eyes on her, the girl deliberately drew her gun, got a clear sight picture, and acquired a few targets. She proceeded to execute a perfect reload as she would have done during the stage and holstered up.

Everyone suddenly realized she wasn't some new shooter we needed to be concerned about.

"Are you ready?" the range officer asked.

She nodded her head yes and settled into her stance while exhaling.

"Stand by..." *Beep*.

Like a seasoned professional, the girl drew her gun, shot the targets and every steel with deadly accuracy, moved within the stage better than the top competition shooters we had there, and made three Green Berets' jaws hit the ground. A thirteen-year-old Amish girl had just smoked us all.

She wasn't big. She didn't look like a CrossFit champion. She didn't have a Special Operations background. She wasn't a man. It sure as hell wasn't the gun she was shooting. I was dumbfounded—partially by the sinking certainty that I wasn't as good as I'd thought.

Why was she better? Like Todd Jarrett, she'd put in the work. She'd dry fired, practiced deliberately, and decided to be good at shooting.

No matter how good you are, there is a teenage girl somewhere who is better than you, and it's because she simply focused on her training and worked harder. That's something everyone can do. Forget about what you think good shooters look like, who they are, or where they come from. The only template that makes good shooters is deliberate, intentional practice. This book will help you understand the concepts of good shooting and sound training so that you can develop a deliberate, intentional practice. Then, maybe next time, you won't be shown up in the field like I was.

1 SAFETY BRIEF

Safety is one of the most important aspects of our training. If you can't perform the drills or general mechanics and handling, then you can't trust yourself to go out onto the range and train to become better the same way those shooters at a high level do. A lot of times, we take safety for granted because we see guys with years of experience who do not appear to acknowledge safety protocols as obviously as newer shooters. They're not as vocal about it. Why is this? Because for them, safety has been ingrained for years. It's automatic and not something they have to preach because it has become the standard in all that they do when handling firearms.

Coaches who have spent years in Special Operations, elite law enforcement, and high-level competitions all include safety as a facet in their training. It's always there and never ignored from the moment a weapon comes out, or they step on the range.

Proper firearms handling for professionals like this doesn't just apply on a flat range—it's also practiced at home while they conceal carry, dry fire, or clean their weapons. The gun is always treated as if it's loaded, and this fact is never compromised. It's never assumed and always confirmed every time you touch a firearm.

FIREARM SAFETY RULES

Below is a list of the minimum basic firearm safety rules, plus a few extra best practices, that will instill good weapons handling. From the moment someone sees you touch a firearm, they should be confident in your abilities to employ it in the manner your training requires. You should have an ego about this subject, in the sense that you always hold yourself to the highest standard. That's an example of ego being a positive for you.

1. Treat all weapons as if they are loaded.
2. Always know the condition of your weapon.
3. Don't put your finger on the trigger unless you are willing to destroy your target.
4. Always know what is in front of and behind your target.

Additional range safety practices:

1. Know your left and right limits on the range.
2. Have a medical plan.
   a. Identify an evacuation vehicle.
   b. Identify the medical bag.
   c. Know the nearest hospital.

3. If you unsling your rifle or unholster your pistol to set it down, clear it and lock the bolt/slide to the rear.
4. Wear eye and ear protection at all times unless all firing has stopped.
5. There is a notional laser coming out of your barrel at all times. Below are the only acceptable directions for it:
   a. The laser is pointed at the sky if in the high ready.
   b. It's pointed at the ground if in the low ready.
   c. It's pointed at a target.
   d. It's pointed down range while scanning/searching for targets.

PISTOL LOADING AND UNLOADING

Loading and unloading procedures are the foundation of proper weapons handling skills. I will say here again that you should never make an assumption about a weapon, and you should always confirm if it is loaded or unloaded. With these steps, if you perform them correctly and in order, you will always know the status of your weapon and be able to confirm it. These procedures were taught to us in the Special Operations community and were briefed and practiced every time we went to the range. From the most inexperienced operator to the most seasoned ones, we all did it. Safety is something never to get complacent with.

Loading

1. Bring weapon up into your workspace in a safe direction.
2. Attempt to place the weapon on safe.
3. Ensure there is no source of feed (ammunition/magazine).

4. Lock slide to the rear.
5. Check three points of contact (those operating parts that a bullet casing would contact), including chamber, mag well, and slide face.
6. Insert magazine, ensuring it is properly seated.
7. Slide forward, observing the chambering of the round.
8. Press check if needed.
9. Bring the weapon down in a safe direction and holster it.

Unloading

1. Bring weapon up into your workspace in a safe direction.
2. Attempt to place on safe.
3. Remove the source of feed.
4. Lock slide to the rear and observe extraction and ejection of the round.
5. Check three points of contact, including chamber, mag well, and slide face.
6. Slide forward.
7. Take one well-aimed shot down range—do not rerack the slide; this way, you know the gun is unable to fire.
8. Bring the weapon down in a safe direction and holster it.

Additional Notes

1. You can modify this protocol slightly to suit your weapon system, but keep in mind these steps will work for all weapons.
2. Every time you touch a firearm, lock the bolt/slide to the rear to observe your three points of contact and confirm that it is loaded. Don't take anyone else's word for it.

3. If you hand a weapon over to someone else on the range to shoot or inspect, state whether it is loaded or clear.

4. Conversely, if someone hands you a weapon to shoot or inspect, ask if it is loaded or clear and then confirm for yourself.

I've seen these steps save several shooters from having a Negligent Discharge (ND) and possibly costing them the shame of irresponsibility, the financial wallop of repairing a bullet hole in their car, or the incalculable impact of ending someone's life. One instance was after a day of training with friends and high-level shooters. Just like we all like to do after the shooting is done and we're packing up, some of the guys were showing off their guns on the back of a truck. There were probably twenty pistols and rifles in the bed, and naturally, everyone was dry firing and handling them. One guy went to pick up a friend's pistol to check out the milled slide and red dot that he'd just added. His friend said it was clear. He picked up the pistol, pointed it in a safe direction, and as he was about to dry fire it down range, he stopped. He remembered what he had been taught and double-checked that there was no mag in the pistol (there wasn't), then locked the slide to the rear. A round ejected. Because he stopped himself and did the right thing, he didn't have an ND. He also didn't have to look around and explain to everyone there whose pistol it was and say, "He told me it was clear." It would have been nobody's fault but his own. He would have been the person who had NDed on the range. Instead, he was the person who did the right thing. It was a good learning opportunity for everyone there and fortunately didn't result in something far worse.

Be the person who sets the standard on the range. It starts with safety and handling, which enables you to do all of the high-speed movement and drills that you need to. Set the standard for others, because chances are, they won't. This is a no-compromise skillset.

2 FUNDAMENTALS

Fundamentals are the primary rules and principles on which shooting, and anything else we do for that matter, are based. There's an old saying in gunfighting circles that there's no such thing as an advanced gunfight. While many of us reading this will hopefully never be in a gunfight, we can learn from the lesson all the same. Whether you've just bought your first pistol or you carry a pistol professionally, mastery of the fundamentals is always the goal.

If we looked at it from a motor learning perspective, which is the study of how we learn movement skills, we would organize pistol shooting into a taxonomy, and the base of that classification system would be the fundamentals. Then we would start to classify skills, like shooting from alternate positions or shooting after moving, by simply layering or stacking fundamentals. We would continue to build the classification of skills based on the complexity that results from stacking fundamental skills. Both perspectives—the practical, lived, applied perspective and the academic, theoretical experience—would come to the very same conclusion: fundamentals are the key to what we typically consider "advanced" shooting. The best-kept secret in the world of performance is the notion that there are very, very few skills that require a specific genetic code to excel at them. Even then, those who have that genetic code still have to study, practice, and train to improve their natural abilities. Pistol shooting, and shooting in general for that matter, isn't one of those skillsets. Everyone can do it, and everyone is capable of being really good at it. The only limiting factors are motivation, effort, and time.

FIRING PLATFORM

The firing platform is a term we use to describe the physical structure we put on and build around the pistol so that we can do two things—be consistently accurate and maintain our accuracy over extended strings of fire. The primary aspect of the platform is that we always move and manipulate the pistol in relation to ourselves; we don't move to accommodate the pistol. We start with the grip because of its obvious proximity to the pistol and then work through the body positions that support it.

The Grip

The way we build our grip around the gun can affect each shot we take. Too much tension, and we overstress; too little, and we can't get the sights back on target in a way that allows us to take rapid and accurate shots. At the same time, we have to train our hands to absorb energy evenly so that the gun returns to the same index point each time instead of landing off to the left or right of where we initially aimed and took our shot.

I have been privileged to attend Special Operations shooting schools, as well as several different professional, military, and law enforcement shooting schools, and in all that time, I have heard the grip explained in at least that many different ways. For the purposes of this book, I'm going to talk about the grip like a three-piece jigsaw puzzle. The three pieces, which we'll discuss in more detail later on, are the pistol itself, your shooting hand, and your support hand. Think of the firing hand as a "platform" and the support hand as the grip, strength, and drive hand. Apart from a solid athletic stance and a basic understanding of the physics of recoil, it's your job to put those pieces together in a way that works best for you.

Firing Hand

One of the most common problems for shooters, whether beginner or experienced, is that they overgrip the gun with the firing hand and, as a result, don't get as high or as close to the bore axis (the axis where the kinetic energy originates) as they need. Usually, this is because the shooter is trying to control the grip with strength instead of leveraging the frame of the gun in a way that locks the wrist, gets high on the bore axis, and allows the trigger finger to move quickly because the firing hand is not under so much tension.

"Spread the gun" is a different way to think about what you should be doing here. The most important parts of the grip are the middle and ring finger, which hook and pull down on the frame, and the first large knuckle of the thumb, which drives up and wraps around the beavertail at the energy-producing axis. To achieve this grip, hold your hand straight out and *hook* your middle finger like it's wrapped around an imaginary frame. You'll notice that the middle finger and thumb knuckle are mostly in line with each other. Now *drive* your thumb knuckle up, pulling down with the middle and ring finger, and feel the wrist *lock* on the bottom. Your thumb knuckle should be a little bit higher up than the middle finger. With guns that have a low bore axis, like Glocks, this technique will help to get the webbing between your thumb and index finger higher up under the beaver tail and closer to the slide. The downward pressure exerted by the middle and ring finger, combined with the upward pull of the thumb, acts to "spread" the gun between those two points of the hand and provide the leverage that allows us to control the gun without fatiguing our grip strength. The test is to check the rate at—and the efficiency with—which you can move your trigger finger. You should be able to move it quickly and independently of the rest of your fingers. Work through this exercise in dry fire until you can start to feel yourself leveraging the gun.

Hook + Drive + Lock = Spread

Support Hand

Most people shoot their pistol with their dominant hand. Ask anyone on a range, and 99 percent of them out there will consider their firing hand to be their dominant hand. In actuality, you should consider your dominant hand your support hand. This is because the support hand is the one doing most of the work. The firing hand is a solid firing platform for manipulating the trigger correctly. As such, it accounts for about one-third of your recoil management. Your support hand (our new dominant hand) actually does the rest of the work and makes the sights reindex back to the original point of aim before the shot was taken. The support hand is, therefore, the main player in the grip, as it drives the gun from target to target and supplies most of the strength applied to the pistol.

In less-experienced shooters, the "grip" typically breaks down after three to five rounds. One reason is that upon taking the first shot, our focus shifts to the trigger finger and sight picture, and we forget about the support hand. You need to keep the focus on your support hand and really feel it *pressing* into the frame and *torquing* forward so that you can mitigate recoil. Lock it in from the start and don't lose that feeling. A good way to develop this feeling is to cup the edge of a table so that your fingers are on the bottom side and your palm is flat on top with the thumb pointed straight out. Now press your hand against the table and apply rotational force forward so that the thumb starts to point forty-five or more degrees away from you. The feeling of tension and friction on your palm is what you should feel on the frame of the gun. It's almost as if the skin is being stretched by the forward torquing of the hand.

Press + Torque = Recoil Management

Recoil on a pistol is straight back; then, when it hits the back of the frame, we get most of the rotation that causes the sights to raise. The firing hand platform *spread* addresses part of this, while the nonfiring hand's TORQUE covers the rest. All you have left to do is to *press* the trigger.

Spread + Torque + Press = Grip

Common Issues

It's one thing to understand good grip on paper. Unfortunately, it's never that easy in real life. I like to compare firing the pistol to performing the snatch. The snatch, if you are unfamiliar, is an Olympic weightlifting movement that is also common to CrossFit. In its most basic form, the snatch involves moving as much weight as possible, as efficiently as possible, from the ground to overhead in one movement without stopping. If one aspect of the maneuver is off, the weight won't be in line as you get it overhead, and you will miss the lift. In the snatch, the lighter the weight, the more room for error you have and vice versa—the heavier the weight, the less room for error you have.

To translate this analogy to the pistol, think of the weight you are lifting as the speed at which you are firing the gun. Slower shooting speeds and a larger target equal more room for error, whereas the smaller the target is in reference to your sights, and the faster you pull the trigger, the less room for error you have. I like this comparison because it gets at the way you have to generate force onto the pistol evenly—much like keeping the weight in line—so that the pistol recoils evenly and returns to the same point. If you apply force in an uneven manner or pull the trigger in any direction other than straight back, then it will affect the gun.

The rifle, on the other hand, is more like a deadlift because it's simpler. To perform a deadlift, simply raise the weight straight up from a bent position to a standing one. When shooting a rifle, lock the gun in with a solid platform and manipulate it as needed, and you'll be successful. The pistol is more complicated because you've got one point of contact—the frame—that you have to exert your force onto to keep the pistol stable. It has to float out in front of you while your two arms act as frames, and force must be applied in an even manner to get the sights back to where you want naturally.

You can diagnose your specific shooting issues by identifying the common problems below:

- Rounds impact inside of your point of aim (left of target for right-handed shooters, right of target for left-handed shooters).
  - Trigger is not being pulled straight back. Find a new reference point where the trigger is traveling at a more outside angle than it was. If needed, put more finger on the trigger and scrape the face of the trigger toward that outside angle.

- Rounds impact high.
  - Quit looking at your target as you are firing. What's happening is that as you go to take the shot, you are looking for the impact of the round on the target. Doing that causes the muzzle to drift up slightly, which makes the round impact high.

- Rounds are impacting low, or you have a hiccup when you are shooting a string of fire.
  - As you shoot, you are most likely developing tension in the torso and bearing down on the pistol instead of pressing through it. The fix is to press the gun out along your line of sight and to think "up and out," not "down and tight."
  - Another cause may be that you are overpronating the firing hand as you shoot. Sometimes we call this

anticipation, which is fairly accurate. Instead, think about holding the torque of the nonfiring hand the entire time and feeling it through your shot string. Start with the required amount of force; don't add or take any away. Put the focus on the nonfiring hand, not the one pulling the trigger.

- As you fire, you are flinching and moving the sights as the shot breaks.
  - Usually, this error is fixed by changing the way you see your sights. Instead of focusing on the front sight and seeing it perfectly crisp like we've been taught, see through the sights with a different focal point. This way, if the sights move slightly as you fire, you won't try and correct them at the last second, which could be causing a minor correction (flinch) as the shot goes off.

Stance

It's accurate to say that there is no such thing as a shooting stance and also that you should have a good stance when shooting on the range. There's no such thing as a shooting stance because, really, all you need to make an accurate shot is sights on target and a good trigger pull straight to the rear so that it doesn't deviate your sights. That said, it's easier to accomplish those things when you're in the right position, and sometimes you're going to have to be prepared to shoot when you *aren't* in your ideal position. For that reason, we want to practice good body mechanics on the flat range so that we can ingrain what good position is. Everything we practice static should translate to movement.

When I first joined the Army and got to my unit, the military was teaching a stance like so: an exaggerated bend forward at the waist, with the shoulders and center of gravity over the balls of the feet. Because we were off centerline and the weight was shifted forward, a lot of shooters would start to shake because their posterior chain was so stressed out and fatigued. All this stance afforded us was another recoil management tool, achieved by bending into the gun. As we've already discussed, though, Press + Torque = Recoil Management. Not only was that awkward position unnecessary; it was actually causing more problems than it was addressing. One thing I noticed was that the guys who shot really well on the move didn't maintain that stance once they started walking and shooting. They moved in a much more upright position, with the shoulders closer to being stacked over the hips (but still slightly in front due to loading the hips).

In other words, there are multiple ways to manage recoil, and anyway, shooting a gun isn't only about recoil management. Giving and accepting force is important, but so are accuracy and speed. For a stance that addresses all these concerns, we have to start with our base.

Base

If you look at top-level fighters in boxing or MMA, you'll notice that they all load their legs. They square their bodies to their opponent, place their feet approximately shoulder width apart (with the strong side, or firing side, foot back), and sink their hips, a position that allows them to generate force. Now they are ready to throw a powerful punch, kick, or sprawl, or shoot in quickly for a takedown. It's also much harder to topple them over than if their legs are straight and they're standing upright because they have a good base. A good example of someone demonstrating a strong base would be Mike Tyson (although he's not an MMA fighter).

The same principles apply to proper shooting stance. We need to square up the torso and hips because we are trying to apply an even force to the pistol. Just like when performing a snatch or a clean and jerk, the hips are what generate power. They strengthen our base, and with a strong base, we can move quickly and powerfully in all directions.

Let's try it. Stand straight up with both feet about shoulder width apart. Imagine there is a plus sign on the ground. The horizontal vector goes directly through the middle of both feet. The vertical line dissects your body into equal halves. Step your nonfiring-side foot in front of the horizontal line and your firing-side foot behind the line. Now sink your hips down a couple of inches by pushing the hips back slightly to load the legs. Make sure your shoulders are generally stacked over the hips, perhaps just slightly in front. This loads the hips and tightens the lower back to create stability. Note: everyone is built differently, so you and I are not going to look exactly the same. If—from this position—you can walk forward rolling heel to toe without changing levels up or down, then you're probably good. Too low, and you look and feel goofy. Too high, and you have no base.

The biggest thing to keep in mind is that the stance should be comfortable, and you shouldn't be stressing out your posterior chain or feel off balance. Remember, hips drive the gun most of the time. As a general rule of thumb, where your hips point, the gun should too.

Frame
The frames, in shooting, are the arms. We are pressing the gun toward the target and driving it between targets. Usually, frames are considered

solid, straight materials that brace a structure. Here, it's the same in theory, except that we don't want to lock our arms all the way out. You have to find that middle ground between arms fully extended and arms too bent or compressed. Too far out, and you will lose the angle of the forearms that allows you to apply rotational force—torque—onto the frame. Too far in, and you won't line up the forearm and upper arm, which will result in the recoil causing the elbow to break too much instead of absorbing the shock.

Long muscles are weak muscles. If your arms are too far stretched out, you can't apply your force to the gun. This is because the straightened forearm is causing the palm to contact the frame in line with the forearm instead of at a slight angle so that you can get a good contact patch. Also, the shoulders will be out of alignment because they are rolled forward too far. The shoulder is strongest when the shoulder blades are in a packed position, meaning the scapula lays flat against the rib cage. Here you will be able to hold the gun out longer without fatiguing due to improper body mechanics. Shooting a pistol is done from the elbows forward. Just relax your shoulders and focus on the elbows pressing, or wedging, the gun forward while pulling your scapulae flat.

To create your frame, set up your base as described above. Hold both hands straight out in front of you in your line of sight. With your fingers open and straight, press your palms together. Make sure your hands are all the way out so that the arms are straightened and elbows locked. Now press your palms together as hard as you can. You can't squeeze them together very hard. Keep pressing them together and start to slowly bring them back from full extension. After a couple of inches, you'll start to feel the pressure on your palms increase as the angle of the forearms decreases. You're stronger here and can more easily manage recoil.

Touch

Touch is the last part of the shooting equation. It has to do with how we pull the trigger, but also with how we touch the target by pulling the trigger. You can also think of touch in terms of concealed carry or contact distance range engagements. If needed, you can "touch" with the arms and hands to create space and an opportunity to draw the gun. Finally, touch affects your base and frame.

With a loaded base and a strong frame, you can leverage the gun more efficiently. The more efficient you are, the less stress you'll place on other parts of your body, and the better you will perform. The better you perform, the more accurately you'll touch the target—which is, ultimately, the goal. Every time you step up to shoot, work through your process of setting your base and framing the gun out and on target, and then see what it feels like to properly touch the target. Practice this sequence enough times before you shoot, and it will become second nature so you don't have to consciously think about it.

Taking all this in may be a bit overwhelming and will definitely take some time to figure out. One thing to remember is that we are all built differently. How I look, or how any other person looks, applying these fundamentals may be different from you. That's okay. Shooting is a journey, one that is constantly refining itself in the name of measured progress. With intentional and deliberate practice, you can start to find out what works for you. Practice at home to find what feels right, then validate it on the range. Remember how each part of the grip and stance feels so that when you do go to train with live rounds, they can become a force of habit. We want the fundamentals to become second nature so that we don't have to think about them when firing. We want them to become automated. Lastly, accept that you will make mistakes and be willing to change to achieve the results you want. To know what right is, you first have to know what wrong is.

3 VISION

Human beings are highly dependent on our sense of sight. Vision is a large part of the mechanism by which we understand our environment, and a significant portion of our brain is dedicated to processing what we see. From a stress perspective, the main function of our vision is to help us determine how alert or activated we need to be in any given situation. Because we are so dependent on our vision, and our visual system is directly tied to our stress response processes, it makes sense that we should train our visual system to improve our shooting performance like we train the rest of our bodies.

VISUAL GAZE

The first concept I'd like to explore is our visual gaze. Wider visual gaze is associated with lower stress levels and better motion detection.

Narrower visual gaze, or focus, is associated with higher stress levels and lower peripheral vision. Think about shooting a pistol: if we need to shoot several targets in a single string of fire, then a wider gaze will serve us better. We'll remain calmer with acceptable sight pictures as we move the sights from target to target, and we'll notice more of the targets sooner. If, however, we need to make one precise shot, then it makes sense that we narrow our gaze into a smaller focal point on the sights. We'll need the boost in stress response to feed the energy demand associated with holding the gun as still as possible while our brain precisely lines up the front and rear sights over the target.

What about when we need to switch between a wider and a narrower gaze quickly? Well, the muscles of the eye are just like any other muscle in the body, in that if we condition them for specific tasks, they will adapt to the conditioning. This is an important aspect of pistol training that often gets neglected. Practice shifting your visual gaze from a wider field to a more focused central vision, and then practice focusing on points farther from or nearer to yourself in space. Your shooting accuracy will increase as your visual control does.

The most typical vision progression in pistol shooting (with conventional iron sights) is (1) we identify the target, (2) we shift our focal plane to our sight alignment, and (3) we refine it to the front sight post. We are taught to have a crystal clear front sight focus because it helps us align the clear front sight with the relatively clear rear sight and the relatively blurrier target. The reason this is the first stage of the progression is that it is the best technique to ensure accuracy. As we are learning pistol fundamentals, we typically can't rely on our grip and overall firing platform to align the sights yet, so we are more dependent upon our visual patterns.

SIGHT ALIGNMENT

Sight alignment refers to the way that we line up the sights on the front (e.g., barrel) sight and the rear (e.g., handle) sight ends of the weapon. It's commonly described as "equal height, equal light" (Figure 3.1), meaning that the top of the front and rear sights are equal, or even, in relation to each other and that there is an equal distance between each outside edge of the front sight and each inside edge of the rear sight. Lining up the sights is easy. Keeping them lined up isn't. Understand that the goal isn't just to line the sights up correctly but to keep them lined up as each shot breaks. Having a red dot helps. After you've assumed the proper stance and built your frame, put the dot on the target before pulling the trigger.

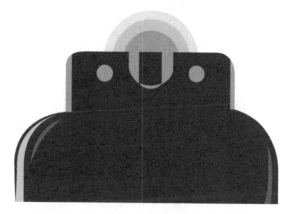

Figure 3.1

Precision and accuracy both improve with correct sight alignment. Precision is when we can shoot a string of bullets that hit the target in nearly the same place. Accuracy is when we can shoot a bullet that hits the target exactly where we want. To shoot an accurate shot, use the sights to determine where the bullet will impact the target. To shoot a precise shot, use the sights so that the bullet will hit the target wherever you choose. Of course, neither of these is possible (with any regularity, at least) without first mastering the fundamentals. The fundamentals allow us to hold the gun the same way, press the trigger the same way, and have the same sight alignment each time so that every round we fire hits the target in the same location.

So how do we use the sights effectively? Assuming our grip and trigger press fundamentals are sound, there are four different techniques for achieving sight alignment. In order of highest to lowest initial precision and accuracy, the four different sighting techniques are conventional sighting, front sighting, backplating, and natural point-of-aim shooting. With practice, a shooter can become equally accurate using any of these sighting techniques, but my experience suggests that the progression outlined here is not only the safest but also the most effective way to learn to be accurate using all four techniques.

Since the conventional sight alignment technique is, initially anyway, the most accurate and precise, it is also the safest. This is important because once the bullet leaves the gun, we can't take it back—so we ought to be accountable for every bullet we fire. To use the conventional sighting technique, acquire a sound grip, align the sights "equal height, equal light," and press the trigger to the rear. When we can repeat these three steps consistently, we will shoot with precision. All the bullets we fire will hit the target in the same place, even though it may not be where we intended them to hit. Precision helps us make the connection between our shooting fundamentals and bullet impacts. When we establish precision, accuracy is a matter of adjusting the sights to move our groups. For pistol shooting with iron sights, this usually means adjusting the rear sight to move the groups left or right and learning elevation holds (that is, knowing the sight height over the trajectory of the round, if it applies, at a given distance) for our particular gun/sight setup.

The second sight alignment technique, front sighting, is what it sounds like: using only the front sight. With practice, we can still be relatively accurate with this technique, especially at short distances and with relatively large targets. If, for example, you're shooting IPSC targets inside ten meters, then it's likely that the front-sight-only technique would be a sound sighting strategy. If you are shooting three-inch dots, on the other hand, front sighting probably won't work very well. As your shooting skill progresses, you can learn to use the front-sight-only technique to get shots on target faster.

The third sight alignment technique is backplating. To use the backplating technique, look at the target and place the square shape made by the back of the frame over the target. The backplate technique is only suitable when shooting at large targets that you need to engage quickly. Because it takes a considerable amount of practice to be accurate using the backplate technique, build a solid foundation of fundamentals first. When you start to use the backplating technique, shoot at large targets at close range and only when you can accurately engage them. From there, slowly start increasing your distance from the target.

The fourth and final sight alignment technique is called natural point-of-aim shooting. Natural point of aim is when we don't look at the sights at all and rely on our ability to align the gun naturally based on how we are indexed toward the target, essentially aligning our body with the target and firing the round. The natural point-of-aim shooting technique can be effective at short ranges; however, it takes the most practice to master and should only be practiced in situations where there is no chance you can hurt anyone or anything around you.

So, to sum up, it's best to focus on the conventional sight alignment technique at the beginning and move on only once you've mastered that technique. Again, because the conventional sight alignment is the safest and most accurate, it serves to ensure that our fundamental practice is sound. Additionally, the more repetitions we get in using the conventional sight technique, the more successful we will be at the other sighting techniques. The other sighting techniques listed allow a shooter to draw their gun quickly and engage quickly. Whether you are in a competition, training or practicing at the range, or in a self-defense situation, knowing what you can hit at different distances and speeds will only add to your skillset. You may not need to use another sighting technique, but it's good to have the option.

NEAR/FAR FOCUS

Whatever sight alignment technique we're using, there are a couple of other things we can do to maximize our success. One of these is to further hone our visual control with near/far focus drills. Like alternating between a wider and a narrower visual gaze, practicing shifting our focus from a near object to a distant one and back again can help refine our shooting accuracy and precision.

Near/far focus is a primary visual pattern, one you've already subconsciously used if you've ever shifted your visual focus from the target (i.e., far) to the sights (i.e., near) and back as you ensure the front and rear sights are aligned with each other and the target. To train this visual system, all we need to do is practice deliberately, as opposed to just occasionally, shifting our visual focus from far to near, near to far. To help you out, I've included a Near/Far Focus Drill in the Appendix II: Drills section of this book.

Most near/far focus drills consist of two identical grids populated with random letters or shapes. One copy of the grid gets posted to a wall. The second, smaller copy you hold in your hand. You begin by focusing on just one letter or shape on the wall grid until you have a crystal clear image of it in your mind. Then you immediately shift your visual focus to the exact same letter or shape on the smaller grid you're holding in your hand.

The drill you'll find in the back of this book is like that, but progressive—i.e., there are multiple stages, each of which builds on the previous stage. Instead of using random letters or shapes, I've listed some common verbal cues used in shooting. Provided you have twenty-twenty vision, you'll start by assuming your shooting stance, at full presentation, roughly five feet away from the grid on the wall (as long as you can clearly see the far grid), with the smaller grid in your hand. As you get better at shifting your near/far focus, you can extend the distance to make it harder to get a crystal clear image of the cues on the wall.

Initially, you'll move through the grid left to right, top to bottom, as you would read. The next progression also starts in the top left corner, but this time, you'll work top to bottom as you move through each successive column. For the last progression, you'll again start in the top left corner but work diagonally down to the bottom right. Finish that, and you'll work from the top right diagonally down to the bottom left. (If you want an extra challenge, try visually hitting the individual letters only, skipping the numbers you've already seen.) Don't expect to complete all three progressions in one iteration. The goal of the drill is to gradually increase the speed at which you can get crystal clear images on both the near and far grids. You'll notice your eyes and concentration will begin to fatigue at some point. Use the fatigue as a guide for future iterations. If you were able to make it through three rows before your fatigue slowed you down, then next time, try for four rows.

SIGHT PICTURE

As your fundamental skills improve, your visual patterns will as well. You'll always look for the target first, but what you'll notice is that as your grip fundamentals improve, you'll start to move from the sight alignment fundamental to the sight picture fundamental. That is, instead of looking for "equal height, equal light" to ensure your sights are aligned on each shot, you'll start to see the front and rear sights as one complete image, or picture, that you're simply overlaying on the target(s). Your near/far visual training combined with dry and live fire grip practice will facilitate this process, and your progression as a pistol shooter will also include a progression in your visual approach. It's part of why the conventional sight alignment technique is so valuable. By training ourselves to use conventional sight alignment, we are ensuring that our grip and stance fundamentals are sound. We know that to be true because when we see the sights aligned and the trigger breaks, we can expect the impact to be where the sights were. If we didn't see the sights, we don't get any feedback regarding our overall shooting platform. When we see the sights, we can diagnose fundamental problems, and we are also setting the conditions to train our vision to be more efficient.

To develop this vision approach, we need to train our binocular visual system to work as a single unit toward the creation of the one-sight picture. Based on readily available information regarding eye dominance, we know that right-eye dominance or left-eye dominance is actually more of an individual preference than a neurobiological fact, which means that we can train our eyes to work together more efficiently. The way to do this is by using a Brock string. The Brock string is strung with colored balls (or knots, if you're making your own) and secured to the wall. While holding the end of the string on your nose, practice shifting your visual focus from the closest ball to the next closest ball, to the next, and so on—then back to the closest. You could—and should—get creative with it and practice shifting your focus between the different balls in different orders and progressions.

A more advanced version of binocular training is included in the Appendix II section of this book. We simply call it the Binocular Focus Drill. It consists of a single black card with two complementary images: a white plus sign on the left side and a red circle on the right (see Figure 3.2). To do the drill, hold the card in front of your nose, then slowly move it away until, with your eyes, you can "move" the two symbols together, putting the plus sign into the circle. You'll actually see three images at first. You'll have the one combined image and then one image on each side of it. Concentrate on the image in the middle and try to move the plus sign around in the circle or the circle around the plus sign. You'll find out quickly that one eye is doing most of the work of moving the shapes on top of each other. Try using the other eye until you can move the plus sign so that all four ends touch the red circle at the same time. Once you've done that, try to keep the plus sign in the circle as you move the card closer to or further from your nose.

The second phase of the Binocular Focus Drill involves merging the shapes together. Once you've done this visually, move the card and your head in the same direction while keeping the shapes merged together. If it helps, think of your upper body like

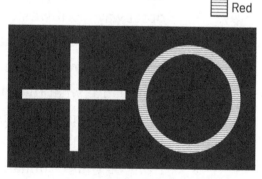

Figure 3.2

a turret, all parts rotating left and right as one unit. Alternatively, you can imagine you are looking through your sights as you scan the room. While we don't want to ever scan for targets through our sights, for the sake of training your eyes to work together, it's a good progression in the skillset.

The third phase is to get the shapes merged together, and this time, keep your head still and move only the card and your eyes. Start by slowly moving the card left and right, then up and down, then diagonally. As you get better, try increasing the range of the movement. The goal is to keep the two shapes as one image the entire time the card is moving. If you can't do that, you're moving it too far or too fast. Think of this exercise as increasing the range of motion for your binocular vision—the wider the area you can cover, the better.

As with the Near/Far Focus Drill, fatigue will be the limiting factor here. When your eyes start to fatigue, shut it down and move on to something else. You can use this drill as an exercise to strengthen the muscles of your eyes, to coordinate the way they work together, and eventually as a warm-up on range days. Vision is a skillset. The more we use it intentionally and purposefully, the better it gets. It works the other way too: if we stop using it, we'll lose it.

A note on eye dominance since it is a common point of discussion on shooting ranges: when someone talks about the "problem" of eye dominance, what they usually mean is cross-eye dominance, wherein your dominant eye is on the opposite side of your body as your dominant hand. If that's the case for you, simply present the sights in front of your dominant eye and slightly turn your head. Doing so will allow you to shoot using your dominant eye while preventing you from needing to change the angles of your fingers, hands, and wrists or anything else about your shooting platform. Another correction is to train yourself to use both eyes equally using drills like the Binocular Vision Drill, shooting with both eyes open, and getting out to the range more often. It will take a significant investment of effort and time, but in the long run, this second correction will likely be a better option.

Training our binocular focus also provides us with a few additional advantages. Primarily, it will help us find our sights faster. Secondarily, it will help us align the sights with targets faster. Once we've trained our eyes to work together better, we can see more than just the sights and the target. The skill of shooting with both eyes open and training them to work together allows us to maintain more visual situational awareness. That is, we can see more of what is going on around us. Maintaining visual situational awareness results in such benefits as reducing target transition time, mitigating the need to "peek" over the sights after single shots, reintroducing the option of using backplating or natural point-of-aim shooting sighting techniques, and generally giving us a better sense of control by allowing us to do what we call "seeing through the recoil." To understand what this last term means, let's now turn to visual focal planes.

VISUAL FOCAL PLANES

So far, most of our discussion regarding vision has been centered on the sights because the skills described above are the most fundamental. Mastery of the fundamentals has to happen before anything advanced can be achieved. Since we know that there's a difference between the visual patterns of novices and experts and that there's a critical path to travel on the journey from novice to advanced, the information in this chapter is presented in the same manner. Now that you understand sight alignment and sight pictures, we can talk about focal planes.

There are three focal planes shooters use. The first is commonly referred to as a "hard sight focus." We call it that because the sights are clear, with clean edges, and the target is blurry. A "hard target focus," on the other hand, means that the sights are blurry and the target is clear. (The Near/Far Focus Drill, by the way, will train your eyes to "hard" focus on each of these planes.) The third and last visual focal plane is called the "50 percent plane."

The name 50 percent plane comes from the idea that, when using it, our focus isn't on our sights (as in the hard sight focus) or on the target (as in the hard target focus) but on some indeterminate point about halfway between the sights and the target. We still use some hard target focus to identify and confirm our target(s) and some hard sight focus to ensure we have an acceptable sight picture; however, when shooting in the 50 percent plane, we are actually looking at a spot between the sights and the target so that we can see the whole picture. There are three reasons to use this approach.

The first reason is that when we have a hard sight focus, our visual system is not capable of tracking the front sight during recoil. It moves too suddenly and too fast. Most shooters I've worked with will talk about experiencing a mental flinch when the gun fires. The mental flinch likely occurs because we rely so heavily on our visual system for input that when we are completely focused on a very small and still object, and then the sights move very quickly and suddenly at the moment of fire, our brains seem to go blank for a split second because we can essentially no longer see anything. The flinch can then cause some other undesirable responses, such as overgripping the gun or jerking the trigger in anticipation.

The second and third reasons to use the 50 percent plane approach are that (1) it allows us to see more of the environment we are shooting in, and (2) it opens our internal focus so that we can feel what is happening in our hands. Both of these things are important for shooters of all types. The more visual inputs we can take in, the more attentional bandwidth we have available to help distinguish the relevant from the irrelevant, in turn lowering our stress response. At that point, tasks like a cadence drill, a plate rack, a shooting competition, or even simple target identification and discrimination become much easier, and we become more efficient at them. If instead, we are constantly staring at a crystal clear front sight post, we will be unable to process the visual information necessary to do any of those things effectively. Finally, when we can start to feel what is happening in our hands, we can adjust our fundamentals to correct for and ensure speed and accuracy.

Taken as a whole, the visual system described above is what allows us to "see through the recoil." In other words, the way we choose to look through the sights at the targets allows us to limit poor trigger presses and resets (more on this in Chapter 4), find follow on targets faster, make more efficient target transitions, and put more effective rounds on target at a faster pace, all without sacrificing accuracy. When we do this, we see through the recoil.

Tip: to check if you are seeing through the recoil most effectively, try finding the "second sight picture." The second sight picture is what we see after the round has been fired and the pistol has cycled. If our fundamentals are sound, our sights will return to our original sight picture. If they don't, then we know we have an adjustment to make in our fundamentals.

SIGHT OPTIONS

Finally, it makes no sense to talk about sight alignment, sight pictures, and focal planes without also mentioning how the various sight options affect these considerations. While all iron sights are pretty much the same physically, they differ somewhat in how they are used. Some sights are all blacked out, for example. Some have a dot front and a blacked-out rear. Some have one dot in the front and two on the rear sight, while others have a U-shaped rear with a dot on the front sight post that fits into that U shape. On top of this, sights can differ in color and size. There are red sights and green sights, tritium sights and fiber-optic sights, night sights, and competition sights. All of them perform the same function, but they all get aligned a little differently. No matter which option you choose, you should still be aiming with the top of the front sight post as it is even with the top of the rear. The front sight should split the target any time your pistol is properly aligned.

Personally, I only use red fiber-optic front sights with a blacked-out rear. Everyone has a different preference; it's just what I have grown to prefer. For me, a red sight stands out more than a green one, and I can pick it up faster in more environments. Green tends to blend in with the grass on ranges or against other green backgrounds. I don't really see the point in night sights since they only work during a few hours of the day. If it's completely dark out, you can't shoot something you can't see, so you are going to need a light to illuminate the area anyway. The advantage of using a light, either weapon-mounted or handheld, is that it outlines your sights really well so that you have a ton of contrast. A lot of people find it much easier to see the sights while using a light, and at that point, you don't see the dots they put on them anyway. As for the rear sight, I like it blacked out. I (and many other shooters) do much better with a blacked-out rear because then the eyes are not trying to line up three dots, and we aren't fighting with our eyes as they attempt to shift focal planes between the front and rear. A blacked-out rear gives you one less thing to worry about.

Something to watch out for is the width of the front sight relative to the rear notch. If the front is too fat, like on a lot of cheaper sights, then it becomes really hard to line up the front and rear sights from left to right. It also makes it harder to pick them up on presentation. Ideally, your front sight should have a good bit of room on each side of it so that you can notice whether the sight alignment is slightly off to the left or right. A simple rule of thumb, but by no means a hard rule, is that if you are at full presentation and you move the front sight to the inside left or right edge of the rear, then the sight should take up about half of the window as you see it through the rear. Less than half, and it becomes hard to notice if the sight is off to the left or right as you are shooting fast or moving. More than half, and you lose the light to each side of the front sight that's crucial for proper alignment. All that said, you can become extremely accurate with sights that aren't ideal as long as you practice and understand what you need to see to be successful.

One final thing to be aware of that not many people talk about is holdover with your irons. Depending on the sight radius and how tall your sights are, you may shoot a little bit low or high at certain distances. For example, if you have a stock Glock 17, which has a sight radius of 6.5 inches, and you replace the front sight with a 0.215-inch height sight, then your rounds will impact 5.5 inches low at twenty yards.[1] We need to make sure we match our front and rear sights properly for the sight radius. Once you do this, the holdover will be minimal but more noticeable if you have suppressor height sights or any tall sights in general.

Irons vs. Red Dot

A few more notes on different sight options, specifically iron sights versus red-dot sights. I grew up shooting iron sights. By "grew up," I mean when I first started shooting in the military, that's what I learned on. I wasn't a kid who had access to firearms or the means to get out and learn to shoot. In the part of Texas I come from, the only focus was football. By the time I got to the military at twenty years old, I had shot a gun one time in my life. In the Army, we started on iron sights, then moved to red dots for our M-4s because red dots are enablers. As in, the red dot enables us to acquire the target faster, see more of the target, and then shoot it easier because we don't have to line up anything—we just have to put the dot on target. For this reason, red dots are an advantage on both rifles and pistols.

I still like to shoot irons quite a bit and probably split my training fifty-fifty between irons and red dots. Some will say that shooting optically sighted pistols (e.g., those with red dots) will hurt your ability to shoot an iron-sighted gun. This is 100 percent false. Shooting a red

---

1   A great tool to figure out what sight height you need can be found on the Dawson Precision website under the "sight math" tab.

dot on your pistol in some ways is harder, and in some ways, it will make you a better iron shooter.

To understand how one will make us better with the other, we need to understand the differences, the biggest of which is how we see with each type of sight. When shooting with iron sights, your eyes are constantly moving as they fight over where to focus. Is your focal plane on the front sight or the target? Is it somewhere in the middle? Are you constantly getting tunnel vision as you shoot and are therefore not as aware of your surroundings? Iron sights can also be harder to see through—period—than red dots. With an optically sighted pistol, you just see a red dot on top of a target. There is no focal shift needed. You can see more with a red dot because the gun and its housing are not blocking out half of the target, as happens with irons. The dot is in the middle of a clear window and allows you to be "head up, gun up, eyes up." Hopefully, the window is clear. If there is a weird blue tint on an optic, I highly suggest purchasing something else if you have the opportunity. Blue tint is a cheaper coating and will wash out targets in certain lighting. Bottom line: red dots make it easier to see while shooting.

At the same time, optics come with their own set of challenges. That little red dot moves a lot more than most people expect and can be a bit of information overload if you let it. There is a lot more feedback while using a red dot than there is with irons. This feedback can be good if you know how to read it, bad if you let it overwhelm you. When shooting with irons, it's always seemed to me that the little movements I see in the sights as they are on target are subtler and less jerky than when using an optic. Think of it like turning up the sensitivity on your computer mouse or video game controller. Little movements all of a sudden become big, shaky, uncontrollable obstacles until you get used to them. The first-timer who switches to a red dot won't be accustomed to that much sensitivity in the sights. It takes time to get used to optical sights, which is probably the reason some people dislike them. It takes time to feel comfortable seeing something different as you shoot.

Once you do feel comfortable, though, there is an advantage to extra feedback in the sight. It makes you more accurate and able to call your shot more easily. If you dry fire with a red dot, you'll notice that the dot will draw a line after each shot if your trigger pull isn't straight. If it's straight, it won't really move or will vibrate over the target. That visual effect is not something you can see very easily with iron sights.

Lastly, shooting with a red dot is going to make you better with your irons and probably get you to the point where you see your irons as one sight like a red dot, not two that are separate. When that happens, you can put more emphasis on speed.

Teaching vision for shooting is one of the hardest aspects to convey to someone. I can't physically take control of your eyes to show you, and I can't demonstrate so that you can see what I can. Like everything else, it's a process that involves a lot of trial and error. Luckily, there are concepts and levels to help you work toward that visual mastery. Once you understand sight alignment, proper sight picture, and how your eyes work, then you can begin to understand how and what you are supposed to see while shooting. As you progress as a shooter, your eyes will get stronger and better able to process information at high speed. Because you can't shoot what you can't see, the visual side of shooting may be the most difficult to master.

4 THE TRIGGER

For kinesthetic shooters who learn by feel, the trigger is the most valuable source of feedback. Many times, I'll ask a student, "What did you see? What did you feel? What did you think?" For the answer of what they felt, usually the response has something to do with how they are gripping the gun or the shock of recoil. Sometimes they confess to feeling nothing at all. That's okay, but we need to get to the point where we are feeling the trigger. More specifically, we need to get to the point where we are feeling the wall of the trigger pull—how our finger is lined up on it, what angle we are pulling it at, and then what happens after the shot.

Great shooters put a lot of emphasis on the trigger pull and what they do as the shot breaks. This is for good reason. As you know, one important element of taking an accurate shot is having our sights lined up. The second, which we'll dive into now, is breaking the shot in a way that doesn't deviate the sights from the target.

To break the shot correctly, you should press and reset. Press is what you feel and do before the shot; reset is what happens after—how you get back to the wall of the trigger after the gun has gone off.

PRESS

A proper trigger press helps make sure your shot is accurate. Pull the trigger correctly so as not to deviate your sights when the gun goes off, and the bullet goes exactly where the sights are pointed at. It's an easy concept on paper that is much harder to execute in real time.

What part of your finger should the trigger be on? Lining the finger up on the trigger is an often overlooked aspect of shooting. There are a few different ways to think about it, but generally, it is very individual. Some people use the joint of the knuckle; some use the pad of the finger. Why? Because everyone's hands are different sizes. If you have shorter fingers, you'll place the trigger farther out on the pad. Larger hands, and you'll most likely move it closer to, or on, the joint of the knuckle. All of it is fine so long as the bullet goes where the sights are. If it doesn't, you need to rethink your press.

It's not as much about where the trigger is but, rather, what you feel. If you have a flat-face trigger on your pistol, then the conventional wisdom is "feel flat, pull flat." If, when you pull a flat-face trigger, you instead feel a hard edge, then you're most likely not lined up on the trigger correctly, preventing you from pulling it straight back for an accurate shot. If, on the other hand, your trigger isn't a perfectly flat trigger (e.g., the dual trigger and trigger safety of a stock Glock pistol, both of which must be deliberately depressed at the same time), you need to think about it differently. In the case of the Glock, the trigger actually has an apex to it, in addition to the safety bar running through the middle of it. So, what do we feel on a trigger like this? We feel the hard line of the safety bar and equal pressure to both sides of that bar. If you feel something flat, chances are you are off to one side of the trigger.

How do I pull the trigger straight back? Most people think they are pulling the trigger straight back when actually they are not. There are a few reasons for this. First, not all triggers are directly in line with our index finger, even when we have a good firing platform with the firing hand. Hold a Glock, or most any other polymer-framed gun, and extend your index finger. It's above the trigger if you have a good, high grip. To get it on the trigger, you need to angle the finger down. Because of this angle, what you think is straight back actually isn't. If you hold a 1911 or Staccato 2011-style handgun, you'll notice that the index finger is closer to being in line with the trigger. This happens because most guns have slightly different grip angles. Some feel more natural than others, and others are steeper and require more ulnar deviation of the hand and wrist. This is why a lot of people find some guns to be more "accurate" than others. It's not really true; it's just how the ergonomic design of the gun allows you to shoot, or prevents you from shooting, with more accuracy. As long as you pull the trigger at the correct angle, the bullet should go where you want it to, provided you don't overtense the firing hand when the shot goes off. Start with dry fire to dial it in, then confirm through live fire.

Which knuckle does my trigger finger bend at? A lot of new shooters tend to pull the trigger and involve the whole finger. This causes the finger to curve to the inside, which in turn causes your shot to go to the inside. The finger naturally bends at the middle knuckle, not the one closest to our palm. You have to separate these two. When you open and close your hand, you'll notice the whole finger moves together with the rest of the hand. If your finger moves like this when you pull the trigger, then the rest of your hand probably does, too. This is what is meant when you hear about the sympathetic response of the hand when you fire. If you can get the first part of the finger to be straight in line with the palm and only move the finger after that, then you are starting to get it. Pull the trigger at the second knuckle, not the first.

When you do pull the trigger—or "take in the slack"—you're going to feel some resistance at some point. This point of resistance is called the wall. If the trigger travels past the wall, the shot will break as it "triggers" the release of the stored energy in the hammer to fire the gun. To familiarize yourself with the wall, hold the gun on a target with your firing hand only. Begin to press the trigger, feel through the wall, then break the shot, focusing either on your elbow, your wrist, or your thumb. You'll know you've correctly pressed the trigger if you see minimal movement in the sight. Think "wall-elbow," "wall-wrist," or "wall-thumb," depending on what feels natural to you. For a lot of shooters with medium- to smaller-sized hands, the elbow works extremely well. I had to tell myself "wall-elbow" for several months to work through pulling the shot low and inside. Then it turned into just "elbow," and before long, I didn't have to think about it anymore. All I had to do was feel the trigger evenly on the pad of my finger and the bend of my finger at the middle knuckle instead of the knuckle closest to the palm.

Why is my shot still pulling? It could be thanks to your pinky finger. Try holding the pistol with one hand, building your ideal firing platform with it, and taking your pinky off the gun. The pinky gets us in trouble because it's the digit farthest away from the muzzle, and as such, it has more leverage to deviate the sights. If you are having anticipation issues or find yourself jerking a round low and inside when you shoot, removing your pinky from the equation while you are dry and live training with one hand can help.

RESET

If the trigger press starts at the wall, the reset ends at the wall. The press makes your shot accurate; the reset allows you to be faster between shots. We now know that we want to feel the wall right before the shot breaks as we press the trigger. We break the shot at whatever angle is required to consistently pull the trigger in a straight direction. Getting back to this starting point is the purpose of the reset.

The trigger reset is half of being what sport shooter JJ Racaza calls "shooter ready." For the shooter to be ready, he has to have the sights back on target and the trigger reset and ready to fire again. Ultimately, you want to be able to break the shot and reset subconsciously. Here's the key: the finger never tells the brain the gun is about to go off. Pulling the trigger is an automated reaction of the eyes seeing the sights on target. If you are having to think about pulling the trigger, then you are probably thinking about having to reset it too. If this is the case, then you are resetting the trigger too slowly. If we reset too slowly, then we are tensing up the hand, and that can cause a host of problems that will end up pulling the shot. Instead, feel the wall, and when the shot breaks, race the reset of the trigger to get back to the wall, prepared to fire again.

The most common issue I see in a trigger reset is pinning the trigger. When a shooter pins the trigger, it's either because he's using too much force to pull the trigger or because he's too slow getting back on the trigger after firing, likely because he's trying to time the reset of the trigger and the firing of the next round. Whatever the reason, these missteps cost a shooter both time and efficiency. If you've ever been told that you're overgripping with your firing hand, anticipating the shot, or jerking the trigger, consider that if you shot faster or more efficiently, there wouldn't be time for these problems to creep in. To pin the trigger or try to time the shot on the reset is to do twice as much work. Does it really make sense to pull the trigger, pin it, then jerk the trigger back again as you are releasing it? No, because those motions complicate and slow down an otherwise simple movement. "Wall-bang" is a lot simpler, and this is what you should think and feel.

For shooters who pin the trigger, you're in luck—I have two suggestions for you. The first is to imagine that there is a rubber band or bungee tied to your trigger finger. It's constantly pulling the finger away from the direction you want the trigger to travel. The pull may be controlled, but the reset is fast. I like to think of this as "my finger doesn't feel the trigger as I reset," which is to say my finger is moving fast enough that it meets the trigger back at the wall. I know a shooter is doing this if the sound of the trigger resetting is masked by the sound of the gun going off. The bang masks the reset.

My second tip is to think of shooting like boxing. A boxer never throws a jab (or any other punch) and leaves it out there only to slowly draw it back. A boxer stays relaxed so he can be fast. The punch snaps out and back to the start. Now imagine if that boxer threw a punch in reverse. His arm would snap back quickly, then travel out away from his body just as quickly. That's what your trigger reset should be like. Reset allows you to be fast, so make sure you're doing it fast.

In summary, the press and reset are the two most important trigger skills. Although they work in tandem, you may need to isolate one skill at a time while you work to master first the press and then the reset. Focus on just the press until you've got it down. When you no longer need to think about it, you can turn your attention to just the reset.

5 MINDSET

Mindset is an undeniably important aspect of performance. The study of it as an academic field—known as performance psychology—is relatively new, and scientists are still learning a lot about how the way we think influences the way we behave. It's worth including here an overview of what performance psychology has to teach us in terms of how we learn skills like pistol shooting, as well as how we later reenact those skills (the performance). As befits any sound training program, we will begin with the fundamentals, then discuss some specific applications of the fundamental concepts.

ATTITUDE

Attitude is the first fundamental concept informing mindset. It's what makes or breaks a great performer or performance. Think about it:

there are very few physical features or talents that result from genetic makeup alone and which can't be developed by those who weren't born with them. Among these traits are height, vertical jump, sprint speed, and (arguably) intelligence. We know these qualities don't, in any meaningful way, make or break a great performer or performance because there are a lot of unsuccessful people who were born with these talents and just as many successful people who weren't. If you study expertise, you'll learn that most "prodigies" are actually a result of early exposure and interest. It takes more than genes or innate talent, therefore, to reach our full potential. The magical mystery ingredient is attitude.

Perhaps you think you know what the term "attitude" means, but do you know how to "do" attitude? We need an operational definition to put it into action. The one I like the best is, "Attitude is a choice we make that determines how we think and act." I like this definition because it means that the choices we make to determine how we think and act are *always* in our control. Notice that I didn't say those choices are easy or simple—just that they're in our control. The corollary of this statement implies that our mistakes and shortcomings are also, by extension, under our control—and if that's true, then we can fix them!

We fix our faults in the same way we maintain our strengths: hard work and effort. I like best the operational definition of effort as "An expenditure of mental or physical power as a means to an end." Almost always, I prioritize attitude over effort because when times are tough (or even when things are going really well), we still need to decide how to handle them first before spending our mental and physical power to get what we want.

Insofar as human behavior is driven by our goals, attitude determines whether or not we achieve those goals. It helps us evaluate how to handle any given situation we may encounter, whether in our day-to-day lives or as part of a performance-related event we have purposely sought out for participation and competition. Understanding and accepting that our success is, then, often tied directly to how badly we want something and how much effort we're willing to put in for that thing will affect how we approach our shooting and ultimately anything else.

Establishing Attitude

If you're still not convinced of the power of attitude, consider that the dictionary definition of mindset is "an established set of attitudes." Because attitudes are situational—meaning, we are constantly making decisions about how to think and act as our environment changes—it helps on a fundamental level to have already established a set of attitudes (that is, a mindset) that colors how we will respond in a particular situation, ideally in a way that promotes our highest good. Find yourself in the same situation often enough, and your brain will make generalities based on which attitudes generate the best results. Choose this same attitude often enough, and it becomes, through repetition, a belief, one that we then use to evaluate the things that happen to us. Accumulate enough beliefs, and you have a mindset—the direct result of the general rules guiding the specific decisions you make about attitudes!

We see this play out in real life all the time. Humans are really good at taking a lot of information and generating general conclusions. It's why biases and stereotypes exist. Though it takes a lot of conscious effort, biases can be overcome, which means that our mindset is not a fixed trait. It will ebb and flow as our experiences do, again because we are constantly making decisions about how to think and act, evaluating the results, and reaffirming or adjusting our beliefs accordingly. What that should tell us is that if we start to receive consistent positive feedback from our decisions regarding how we are choosing to think and act, it will start to affect our mindset, thereby making attitude the most important factor in our practice and performance.

You may, of course, have different mindsets for different situations. You may have one general mindset for everyday living, one for training, or one for competition. These mindsets can be managed effectively so long as you deliberately develop them for specific purposes and maintain enough mindfulness to recognize if and when a given situation deviates from the norm.

Modes of Mindset

Let's turn now to four specific attitudes that, when mixed and matched, create three basic mindsets in the goal-oriented individual.

The first attitude is called Development-Focused and describes a primary goal of learning and improving. When we have this attitude, we seek out challenges, maintain high effort expenditures, and enjoy competition. We also pass less judgment on our character or identity and really focus on our performance. In other words, we separate who we are from what we do. When we make mistakes, we don't think of ourselves as bad shooters; we simply evaluate what went wrong, make an adjustment, and move on to more practice. Having this attitude promotes resilience, as our measures of success move from solely outcome-based markers to more process- and performance-based indicators.

The second attitude is called Win-Fixated because when we have this attitude, our primary goal is to outperform other people. We are generally prepared to demonstrate high levels of competency in terms of winning and will often stop at nothing—including intimidation, cheating, and other gamesmanship strategies meant to give us the advantage—to make sure we do. In competition, the win-fixated attitude is beneficial because it promotes thoughts and actions that lead to what it will take to win—right now. Effective planning, strategy and skill selection, and higher performance intelligence all result from the win-fixated attitude. At the same time, if we carry this attitude into training, it can also lead to stagnation. If we have to "win" all the time, we'll never address the contextual interference (which we'll discuss in detail later) necessary for learning and improvement.

The third attitude is called Doubt-Oriented, and it is the most complex of the four attitudes. It is also the attitude most easily construed as "negative," since when we have this attitude, our primary goal is to protect our reputation or identity. Having this attitude will prevent us from taking risks necessary to perform well in competitions. In training, those with a doubt-oriented attitude are more likely to practice skills they are already highly competent in and not challenge themselves to refresh previous skills or learn new ones. On the positive end of the spectrum, this attitude can be a sound source of motivation and excitement that helps us focus on expecting the skills we've prepared in ways that maximize their potential.

The fourth attitude is called Failure-Evader because it's all about avoiding any perceptions of incompetence. When we have this attitude, we are likely to define success in terms of avoiding failure, which immediately stunts growth and ultimately prevents us from taking any chance that might result in us looking bad—or worse, proving that we are not competent. From a training perspective, this attitude is completely debilitative, as we'll never learn anything new. From a competition or war-fighting perspective, the failure-evader attitude will steer us away from competitions or gunfights we think we can't win, ironically setting us up to fail before we even try. In the military and law enforcement world, the failure-evader attitude can save lives. For the rest of us, it is almost universally debilitative.

Development-focused, win-fixated, doubt-oriented, and failure-evader. Now that we understand these four attitudes let's discuss three common mindsets created by blending them together (see Figure 5.1).

The first mindset scores high in the development-focused and win-fixated quadrants and low in the doubt-oriented and failure-evader quadrants. For ease of understanding, we call this the development-focused mindset. It's a beneficial mindset in general and the preferred mindset for most of our training and practice sessions, as we feel motivated to perform well but are at the same time interested in acquiring new skills. We want to do our best, but we can stay humble about it and are open to trying different techniques and approaches even if we might not do them well at first.

Next is the failure-evader mindset, which, as the name suggests, scores high in the doubt-oriented and failure-evader quadrants and low in the development-focused and win-fixated arenas. With the failure-evader mindset, we're unlikely to choose to experience anything new or that we fear we won't immediately excel at. Although we might prefer never to have this mindset, it's important to understand from both a conceptual and a practical perspective, as only when we know what markers to look for can we catch ourselves in the act and adjust appropriately.

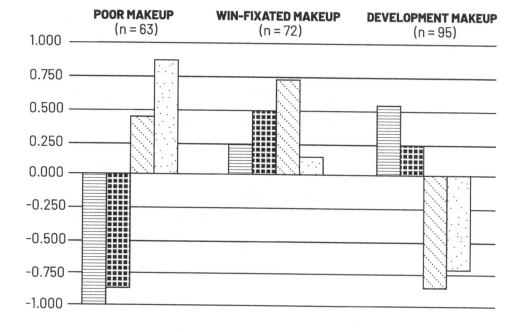

Figure 5.1

Finally, there's a more middle-ground mindset that scores high in the win-fixated quadrant, moderately in the development-focused quadrant, moderately to high in the doubt-fixated quadrant, and low in the failure-evader quadrant. I like to think of this as the competitive mindset. Having this mindset primes us for winning, as with high markers in both the win-fixated and doubt-fixated arenas, we are both motivated to perform well and uncertain that we will be able to repeat our best practice performances. That is, we go into the event with a healthy level of desire to do our best while acknowledging that we might not. Even though the outcome of the competition is unknown, the fact that the failure-evader attitude is taking a backseat in this mindset means that we won't give in to the fear of that unknown but will feel motivated to emphasize our strengths and compensate for our weaknesses—a winning combination if ever there was one!

In reality, the number of possible mindsets generated by combining different degrees and iterations of attitudes is much greater than three. It's practically limitless. These three checkpoints along the continuum are nevertheless enough to outline a framework that we can then use to develop and maintain the mindset that best works for us in any given situation. Step one is becoming aware of the different attitudes and mindsets; step two is putting them to work for you.

VERBAL CUES

The manner in which we talk to ourselves matters. If we consider the classic example of the glass being half full or half empty, we have two perspectives—positive and negative—but we don't have the truth of the matter. All we know is what the relative amount of water means to us. If we see the glass as half empty, we'll be focused on what we don't have with no way to get more of it. If half full, we'll see that we have some water, which is better than no water, but we'll also recognize that the glass is capable of holding much more water, and we still don't have a way to get more. It's only when we adopt a value-neutral mindset that we can see the truth of the matter: regardless of the amount of water in the glass, the glass first and foremost is a container to hold water from a source, and the value of a glass is that it's refillable.

We are prone to negative thinking because of the negative feedback we've received throughout the socialization process of growing up.

Your homework always came back with the number wrong written on the top instead of the number correct. Your parents always told you what not to do before telling you what to do. Your teachers and coaches always focused on what you needed to improve over what you did well. That's okay—there's not a conspiracy to make everyone think negatively all the time. What happens, though, is that because we all have expectations for ourselves and others (expectations that don't need to be reinforced when you've repeatedly met or exceeded them), the sheer volume of negative feedback we receive when we don't meet or exceed expectations tends to automate negative thinking. It's the same premise as "muscle memory," where if we repeat the same movement enough, it will become automatic. Our thoughts work in a similar way: the thoughts we have most often become automated. Therefore, it makes sense that we should train ourselves to think as positively and constructively as possible.

The first step in retraining the "verbal cues" we give ourselves is to be aware of our most frequent and most impactful negative thoughts. Because negative thinking is easily automated, it's difficult to notice, but it becomes easier to spot when we familiarize ourselves with the most common types of negative thinking. Here are the categories they fall into:

- **Being the Critic**. This is the internal voice that judges your performance, prompts you to compare yourself to others, sets impossible standards, and blames you for falling short.

- **Catastrophizing.** When we catastrophize, we tend to expect the worst and exaggerate the consequences.

- **Overgeneralizations.** These happen when we make conclusions based on insufficient evidence without considering the context. Another term for this category is "jumping to conclusions."

- **Blaming.** This is when we blame other people or external circumstances for the results of our performance.

- **Mustification.** If things "must" be a certain way for you or other people, then you're erroneously applying concrete rules that everyone should follow with no deviation, even though, in reality, these "musts" get you no closer to your goals.

- **Polarizing.** Thinking in terms of all or nothing leaves us with little to do about maintaining the all or adjusting the nothing.

- **Perfectionism.** When we think we can't do anything until we can do it perfectly, we seldom get anything done at all.

- **Fear of Failure/Success.** When we fear failure, we focus our thoughts on all the ways things can go wrong. When we fear success, we become irrational regarding perceived expectations of future performances.

- **Social Approval.** When we are focused on how others might perceive us, it distracts us from living up to our potential.

- **Equity.** When we focus on fairness, the scale is almost always skewed against us. Equity teaches us to limit our effort, so we always have an out.

- **Social Comparison.** When we compare ourselves to others and their performance or ability, we struggle to perform well ourselves.

Once we catch ourselves in a negative thought pattern, the next thing we should do is to change our verbal cues to sound beliefs and positive counterarguments. These generally fall into four categories:

- **Self-affirmations.** These are thoughts we already believe to be true about ourselves. They often concern characteristics that lead to consistent practice and performance.

- **Goals.** These are thoughts that help us focus on where/how/ who we want to be, even if we don't really believe we're capable of meeting them yet.

- **Attributions.** These are thoughts we use to explain our performances, both good and bad. Use attributions with care, as we don't want to end up with fundamental attribution error bias (discussed in the next chapter).

- **Appraisals.** These are thoughts we use to adjust our perception of events to see them as challenges we can overcome instead of threats that will defeat us.

With practice, these thoughts become cue words to help guide our focus and reframe our thinking when needed. The list that follows includes some proven guidelines for developing these thoughts as efficiently and effectively as possible:

- **Be as neutral as possible.** You're better off being positive than negative, but if you can train yourself to be constructive as well as positive, you'll always find a course of action. Emphasize your strengths, remembering that one of them is that you control your attitude and effort.

- **Be realistic and objective.** Stay grounded and monitor your progress. The goal is to improve a little every day.

- **Be in the present.** The past only exists if we let it. Use it selectively to recall times when you were at your best and the lessons you learned when you weren't. The future is created by the actions you take now, so there's no sense in worrying about it and not doing anything to influence it.

- **Perceive all things as challenges.** Decide you can overcome anything first. Then evaluate the risks, resources, and consequences to determine if you should.

- **Focus on the Process.** The process is what creates the outcome. It doesn't make any sense to make a plan that ends in failure.

- **Know what you control.** There are essentially three types of things in the world—the things you can always control, the things you can never control, and the things you can't control but that you can influence. Train your thinking accordingly.

- **Separate who you are from what you do.** Good shooters miss; they make mistakes, miss draws, and fumble reloads. They're good shooters because they make practice plans, systematically improve their performances, test their performances, and repeat.

As you become more aware of your negative thinking and the techniques helpful in retraining your thinking, the next step is to make "retrain my verbal cues" part of your daily training, like you would with shooting training or anything else. Adding it to your daily training routine can be as simple as detecting negative thoughts and reframing them into challenge-seeking, constructive thoughts. It can also be as complex as writing scripts of thoughts to practice aloud using the constructive thinking guidelines above. You can write a script for any situation you are anticipating or for a general situation to increase your performance in all aspects of life. Either way, retraining your verbal cues teaches you to perceive weakness as a challenge and guides the successful execution of skills.

6 PERFORMANCE

ABCS OF PERFORMANCE

Our overall goal in training is to develop a repeatable process that produces predictable results. The more consistently we can perform the movement mechanics and performance processes of our shooting, the more accurately we can predict the outcomes. When we can learn to connect the performance processes to the outcomes, we can make more effective plans for performance in new environments and make more accurate adjustments when our results don't meet our standards. Our targets no longer tell us if we are good or bad shooters; they simply give us feedback regarding our performance.

The ABCs of performance begin with an "activating" event—the A in ABC. The event could literally be anything. Some common examples in shooting include a novice shooter anticipating the shot, going downrange to check your targets when you're shooting with your friends, an inexperienced competition shooter stepping up to the starting position and waiting for the beep of the shot timer, or an experienced competition shooter preparing for a stage that includes a swinger, Texas star, or some other type of target array that usually gives them problems. The activating event is going to be different for all of us. The important thing is that we start to recognize these events for ourselves.

The reason they are termed "activating" is that they trigger "belief" systems—the B in ABC—as we evaluate how the event will affect us. Belief systems can be explicit, such as "I suck at shooting swingers," or implicit, taking the form of a general feeling of anxiety because people are watching. The reason we want to be aware of our activating events is that it helps us become more aware of the belief systems we attach to them. The interaction between the event and our belief systems produces emotional as well as physiological consequences.

The "consequences"—the C in ABC—are what we use to mark the experience, and they, in turn, reinforce the belief system. When we connect a consequence to an outcome, the belief system is solidified. The outcome here is the hit or miss, win or loss. The consequence is the emotional or physiological response that results from the way we perceive the event interacting with the belief system we attach to it.

We have all experienced this process. We've all experienced times when we were nervous, anxious, or scared and didn't perform as well as we could have. We've also all experienced times when we were excited, challenged, and motivated and performed better than usual. The lesson the ABCs of performance teach us is that there are very few things we value that are inherently threatening. The situation itself is "value neutral." We bring the judgments with us and apply them to the situation.

Perceiving things as having neutral value allows us to see them for what they are. Then and only then can we start to evaluate our belief systems. When we can train ourselves to evaluate activating events rationally—without bias, just getting to the facts—we start to do two important things. First, we gain a sense of control over the situation, which is one of our strongest stress managers. Second, and a much more difficult feat to accomplish, we start to see the irrationality in our belief systems. When we can do both things, we start to grow.

Outlining the performance process in this way provides us a framework for both awareness and training purposes. It helps us be more aware of activating events. When you start looking for them, you'll find them everywhere, in all aspects of your life. Using the ABC framework also helps us identify irrational beliefs, such as "I just can't shoot swingers," which we can then use to create training goals. The first step is to analyze the belief: "Is there anything about me that's different from other people who can shoot swingers, which prevents me from being able to do it? Do I just not have the time, or do I not make the time? Is it not that important to me to figure out, or is it really that I just can't do it?" There are a lot of reasons shooting a swinger could be difficult, but very few of them have to do with your potential. Recognizing the subconscious roadblocks you might be setting up for yourself can make you more confident, more resilient, and less anxious. The shooter who's identified and challenged his beliefs makes better decisions and lives a more rewarding life. It makes him a better shooter too, because after he's figured out all the reasons why he can't shoot a swinger, he has a precise list of all the things he needs to practice so he can.

FOCUS

Focus is one of the defining factors of elite performance. If you think about all the great performances you've ever witnessed and of the times when you've been at your best, I'll bet that high levels of focus were present in each. In my experience as a teacher, coach, and consultant, I've found that a lot of people are told to "pay attention" or to "get focused," but very few are told how to do it. The concept that has worked best for me is to start by describing attention as "our ability to notice everything around us, as well as inside of us, at the same time." Military and law enforcement refer to this concept as "situational awareness," as it encompasses not only what we notice but also what those things mean to us.

Attention is the mechanism by which we can tune in to a lot of things at the same time. Up to a point, the more we can notice, the better we should be able to process. Noticing too many things at the same time or the wrong things at the wrong time, however, will result in poor performance. We need something to direct our attention, which means we need to know what's relevant and what's irrelevant before we can prioritize these various inputs in terms of importance. This is the process of becoming focused. If attention is your ability to notice everything in and around you, then focus is your ability to disregard what's not important and only direct your attention toward what is important. For a great example of focus, consider that every time you open your eyes, you see the sides of your nose. How often do you notice your nose, though? Hardly ever, right? Focus allows us to disregard our nose because it's not important in the moment. Concentration is the ability to maintain focus over time.

Realizing what you're attending to—or what you're focused on—makes for efficient training progressions. It also gives you a vehicle to reduce distress because when you understand that you're worrying about things that should not, or will not, influence your performance, you can choose to focus on something more constructive instead. An easy way to check yourself any time you start to get frustrated, anxious, or frankly too comfortable with your performance is to ask, "What's important now?" (WIN). The acronym WIN has been a successful tool for athletes, students, operators, and even eight-year-old Little Leaguers. When you know that the answer to the question "How do we spell win?" is "What's important now!" you're on the right track.

GOALS

In order to develop sound belief systems and determine what's important to focus on, we need to have one or more performance goals. The primary reason setting goals is an effective strategy for change is that completing the goal-setting process provides us with focus for our range time. First, we need to determine what it is that we want to change or improve. In shooting, it is often an isolated shooting fundamental or several fundamentals stacked to create an applicable skill. The next step is to identify barriers and construct action plans specifically related to achieving the goal. Common barriers include making time to get to the range, ammunition budgeting, getting targets, and things of that nature.

There are three types of goals we should consider setting. Outcome goals focus us on outperforming another person or standard. A simple example of an outcome goal would be to hit the A zone of the target.

While most of our goals will be written in terms of outcomes or what we want to be able to do, outcome goals are not generally the best for performance. If you were in a shooting competition and decided to make an outcome goal to win the stage, it would not be a very effective way to organize your thoughts and behaviors. Even if you did win the match, you wouldn't know *why* you won the match, and most likely, you would not be able to repeat the performance nor predict your ability to win other matches. The appropriate venue for outcome goals is practice or training sessions during which you are working on a specific fundamental or skill when the outcome you desire is a direct reflection of what it is you are trying to accomplish.

Process goals, on the other hand, are all about improving techniques, mechanics, and strategies for skill development. For a novice shooter working on accuracy with iron sights, an example of a process goal would be to verbalize "equal height, equal light" before every shot. A competition shooter hoping to win the stage would set process goals that mimic the skills needed to complete the competition—skills like the draw, the reload, moving in and out of shooting positions, and shooting accurate strings of fire at multiple targets. In practice sessions, he might focus on getting 10/10 clean reloads (meaning as soon as you feel the recoil of the slide lock, your nondominant hand moves to the new magazine, gripping it between your thumb and middle finger—with your index finger running the length of the magazine—at the same time your firing hand rotates to hit the magazine release and position the mag well so the nondominant hand's pointer finger can point the magazine cleanly into the mag well and seat it as it torques back into the shooting grip). Process goals help us break down outcome goals like winning a stage into smaller, repeatable processes.

Once you've begun to master the skillsets needed to achieve your outcome (or long-term) goals, you should introduce performance goals. Performance goals offer a more objective measure of how efficiently you can complete a skill by encouraging you to time your process goal repetitions. After several iterative performances, you'll establish a baseline time in which you can consistently meet a given process goal. In the slide lock reload example above, you would first establish your baseline, then set a performance goal that's 5–15 percent faster than your baseline. If it took you 2.5 seconds per repetition to get 10/10 clean reloads while focused on the process of the reload, then your first performance goal could be to get 10/10 in 2.4 seconds (a 5 percent improvement) or 2.1 seconds (a 15 percent improvement).

Conceptually, the outcome goals represent our ultimate destination, while process and performance goals represent the paths we take to get there. Remember that where we start means much less than where we end. If it takes you five seconds per repetition to do a clean slide lock reload, then, for now, it takes you five seconds. Putting a systematic goal-setting process in place will make your journey down the path of excellence much more efficient, provide you with sustainable self-confidence, and make your practice sessions and competitions more enjoyable and rewarding.

EVALUATING PROGRESS

The combination of short-term goals (i.e., process and performance goals) and long-term goals (i.e., outcome goals) works best when you add three more tools for success. The first tool for success is to monitor your progress. The addition of a notebook to your range bag may be the most valuable piece of equipment you bring to the range in terms of your personal development. The notebook should contain your long-term goal and all the process and performance goals you intend to meet along the way to achieving the desired outcome. (The drills at the back of this book, by the way, can inform your process and performance goals.) Your efficiency will increase when you take the time to record your results. If you're working on the process goal of getting 10/10 clean reloads, then you're noting the time it takes for each one and making notes regarding problems you've identified and strategies that work.

By consistently monitoring your work, you set yourself up to evaluate your progress. The purpose of evaluating your progress is two-fold. First, you'll hold yourself accountable to making your range time both focused and goal driven, which will support the attention needed for learning and improvement. Second, you'll have an objective perspective of where you stand on your path to success. Objectivity is crucial since it prevents what is known as the fundamental attribution error bias, or a bias that prevents us from seeing the truth of our performance, to which we are all susceptible. What happens when we succumb to fundamental attribution error bias is that we see how close we are to the goal and quickly come up with reasons, attributions, and excuses for why we didn't make the time, accuracy, or other performance goals we were attempting. We do this because we often connect our performance to our character or identity—the same reason it's easier to more accurately evaluate someone else's performance than our own. The threat, of course, is that we leave feeling disconnected from our work or with a skewed sense of confidence—usually inflated—and ultimately, our progress stops.

To retain an objective perspective, we use the third tool for success: managing goal difficulty. Because the goals you set for yourself are yours and yours alone, you're in control of them, and you decide how difficult they are. Growth goals are the simplest and easiest goals to achieve. They're best reserved for learning or relearning a skill because, while they provide the foundation for our skillsets, we don't usually get much back in the form of a real sense of achievement. The second level of goal difficulty pertains to realistic goals, which is what we generally call goals falling into that 5–15 percent improvement range. It may not sound like much, but if you can improve 10 percent every time you go to the range, it won't take long before you're significantly better than when you started. The most difficult goals are called dream goals and describe a level of performance that can only happen when everything falls into place. While there is some value to pursuing a dream goal occasionally, it's generally detrimental for practice and performance because there are too many variables outside of your control, the exact conditions of which aren't typically repeatable. Dream goals tend to distract from your focus, making your development less efficient and increasing your anxiety during performance. When we follow the process to performance to outcome goal concept, we're more likely to achieve a dream performance, almost on accident, than we are to achieve a dream level performance predicated on getting lucky.

Set realistic goals, monitor your progress, and evaluate that progress often. Only then can you retool your process as needed and consistently improve your performance, because you're in control of your own development.

MENTAL REHEARSAL

There's a powerful mental tool we can use to help us progress more quickly. Mental rehearsal is the process of practicing our skills in our head. You've probably heard it referred to as "visualization" or "imagery," and it's the same thing. I like to think of it as "mental rehearsal" because I've found it more accurately describes what this tool is, how it works, and how to use it.

Mental rehearsal works on a concept known as "functional equivalence" or the idea that thinking about something activates the same areas of the brain as actually doing that thing. It has also been demonstrated to increase force output among research subjects taught to visualize their arms as steel beams and benefit rehabilitation from injuries among patients taught to mentally complete strength training exercises. The best part about mental rehearsal is that you already do it almost constantly. All we have to do to take advantage of this tool is to use it on purpose, for a purpose.

To use mental rehearsal effectively, the first thing we need to practice is control. We need to control the images we create so that we are visualizing our mental performance exactly as we want to do it in real life. You'll likely start by creating images in the third-person perspective, as though you're watching yourself in a movie. As you become more practiced at this skill, you can then try mentally rehearsing in the first-person perspective, the perspective that replicates individual experience. At first, the chances are good that you will see yourself fail. It's okay and will actually feed the progression. However, it's not okay to repeatedly see yourself fail. Since you are generating the image and are in control of it, all you have to do is use your own instant replay to see yourself handling the situation or performance in the way you'd like to do it. In the heat of the moment, we will do whatever we've practiced the most, so be sure to complete your mental rehearsals in the ideal state, even if you don't believe you can do something that well or that fast or that accurately. See it happening the way you want.

The first stage of mental rehearsal involves visualizing a skill with which you're already completely familiar. Draw on all of your senses in the image, including your mood and emotional state. Feel the stippling on the pistol grip dig into your hand. Feel the impulse of the recoil as the slide glides over the firing platform. See your sight picture adjust as the slide ejects the brass and your vision snaps back to the original sight picture. Smell the burning powder and the hot gun oil. Hear the muffled sound of the round being fired. See the targetry and layout of the range you'll be shooting at or one you've shot at before. Feel the sunshine or the cold rain. It won't take long to put yourself there with a little practice.

The purest form of mental rehearsal you've probably experienced is at bedtime in that space between being awake and starting to dream. Your body suddenly jerks into action—the same action you were dreaming about. What happened was that your brain confused the reality of you lying in bed and trying to sleep with the reality of whatever you were dreaming about. You were there, in your dream, even though you were actually lying in your bed. While it will take considerable practice to generate images that feel that real in mental rehearsal, eventually, you will achieve the same image quality as you train toward the ideal.

The second stage in the progression is to imagine a situation you're training for in which an unexpected mistake happens. In competition, this will usually be a malfunction or a blown stage plan, but it's your training program, so use the mistakes most common to you. For defensive purposes, you can imagine an unexpected confrontation. See yourself handling either the mistake or the confrontation exactly the way you would in an ideal world, including all your senses and emotions. Rehearse this scenario multiple times.

The third stage in the progression is to imagine a situation where the pressure is on you to perform. Pressure is an individual phenomenon; everyone will perceive it differently. It could be anything from making a rookie mistake at your first competition or training event to a life-or-death decision made by a military or law enforcement team. Whatever you perceive as pressure, rehearse putting yourself in that situation and handling it exactly as you would want to handle it when the bullets are real.

You can, and should, also use mental rehearsal in your daily training. Every drill included in this book has focus points. Visualize yourself performing the focus points of each drill before you actually shoot the drill. Doing so will not only increase your attention, which is vital to learning (especially in adults over twenty-five years of age), it will also improve your performance and train you to visualize and rehearse in other aspects of your performance and life in general. It becomes a forcing function to train yourself to be confident.

CONFIDENCE

Confidence is oversold in two regards—first, as something that is necessary for elite performance and, second, as a feeling that you either have or don't have. Confidence is not necessary for elite performance, at least not in the way we generally think of elite performance. While there's little doubt that being confident helps us perform at higher levels, there's also little doubt that having too much confidence hurts our performance. Because of this paradox of sorts, thinking of confidence as a feeling just isn't that helpful, even though the only way we really experience confidence is as a feeling of willingness that results from our estimation of the outcome.

The first thing we need to do to improve our confidence is to shift our focus from outcomes to performance. We shouldn't be interested in whether or not we can achieve the outcome goal; we should be estimating the probability of being able to perform up to our potential in the current environment. If our training is sound, we should already have a relatively accurate estimation of the probability of the outcome. For example, if the outcome goal is to win the match and three Grand Master-level shooters are there who can execute their process faster and more accurately than we've been able to do during our training, it's easy to estimate that the best outcome we can achieve is fourth place. Instead of focusing on all the reasons why we can't win (since, after all, we're there to compete regardless of how confident we feel), what we should be focused on is how the environment will affect our ability to perform the skills we've trained. If we've trained hard, we can enter any situation feeling confident.

Another way to think about confidence is as an interaction between the variables of preparation and competence. If we start evaluating the activating events through the lens of our relative levels of preparation and competence, we'll make more accurate estimations of how well we are going to do whatever it is we are about to try. Ultimately, what we're doing is training our belief systems to be performance-focused, which will, in turn, produce more helpful psychological and physiological consequences.

Preparation

We'll start with the variable that we have the most control over: preparation. Preparation includes the three subcomponents of physical, social, and emotional preparation. Physical preparation is centered on our fitness and equipment. Our physical fitness will prove to be the most important aspect of our performance in terms of achievement, but also in terms of sustainability, consistency, and repeatability. Equipment falls under physical preparation because, in order to perform in shooting, we need to have the necessary equipment. We not only need to have it with us, but we also need to know how to work it, how to fix it, and when to use it appropriately.

Social preparation concerns the meaning we attach to who we are performing with, who we are performing against, and who will be watching us do it. Who we are working with, competing against, and who is watching (or will know) are largely irrelevant compared to the meanings (i.e., beliefs) we ascribe to these people. Taking the time to consider this prior to participation helps us determine more refined priorities and drives our focus to what we can control—our performance. When we start to understand that we ourselves are creating a lot of the pressure and anxiety we feel, these feelings will dissipate, freeing us up to focus unburdened on our performance.

Emotional preparation can be the most complex because of the nature of our emotional system. Our emotional system is automated in that we don't get to pick the emotions we experience; however, we can train ourselves to regulate our emotional system and respond to our emotions with more effective behaviors. During preparation, we aren't concerned with how emotional we feel or which emotion we are experiencing. What we are focused on is why we are experiencing it. When we understand why, we can address it by looking for the neutral value and shifting our belief systems—or we can reevaluate our strategies for approaching the situation.

Overall, when we are prepared physically, socially, and emotionally, we are ready. When we are ready, we are more willing to perceive activating events as challenges as opposed to threats. We are more likely to switch strategies and keep working than quit. We are also more likely to enjoy and learn from our experiences. Physical, social, and emotional preparation sets the conditions for performing to the best of our ability.

Competence

If preparation is the soft component of confidence, competence is the hard component. It consists of skills, techniques, and strategies. Like preparation, competence is also in our control, though it takes more time to determine and develop. Therefore, it is more productive to think in terms of preparation first, competence second. Doing so will make our training more efficient, as we'll have a clearer understanding of the skills, techniques, and strategies we need to focus on to achieve our goals.

Skills include anything we can learn as a product of effort, repetition, and time. Techniques allow us to vary our skills to adapt to the situation. As we determine the probability of achieving our goal, the first thing we need to know is if we have the necessary skills. If we do, then we need to determine our techniques, or how we'll use our skills to solve the problem. If we don't, then we need to determine which skills we have that will serve us best in the situation, followed by which techniques we'll use. Not only does this maximize our ability to perform, but it also feeds our training program by identifying new skills and techniques to develop and improve.

A strategy is a course of action we can use to solve a problem, perceive a situation, or approach anything we encounter. After we've assessed which resources (i.e., skills) we can use and all the ways we can use them (i.e., techniques) to solve the problem, we need to think of at least two different ways to put our skills into action. Having more than one strategy is imperative. Strategy switching is the key to resilience and mental toughness. If we only have one approach or strategy, and for whatever reason, it doesn't work, we are out of options, and we fail. If we can train ourselves to consistently develop multiple strategies, we always have an alternate way to overcome the challenge.

Confidence, then, stems from our ability to accurately predict our levels of success. In order to predict outcomes effectively and consistently, we need to understand how our preparation and competence work together. Following the relatively simple process outlined in Figure 6.1 is a good way to start developing your own system of building confidence in a way that feeds both your training and performance.

Figure 6.1

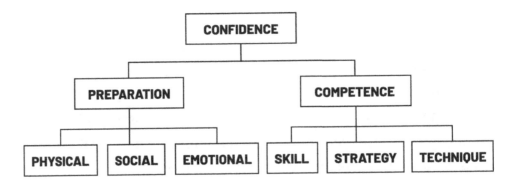

FALSE AND INFLATED CONFIDENCE

If you've ever felt really confident and failed, you know it's a tough pill to swallow. The good news, though, is that now you should have some knowledge to help prevent you from repeating that experience. If you were prepared but not competent, you experienced what is referred to as false confidence. We fall into this trap when our training isn't monitored and evaluated effectively. Our skillsets just aren't as good as we think they are because without an objective measure of performance goals, we are influenced by fundamental attribution error bias, where we only see how close we are when we make a mistake or don't perform to a given standard (vs. making character or global judgments on others' performances). With false confidence, we are quick to think of all the justifications for our poor performance while thinking of others as lazy or just plain bad shooters.

If your competence was high when you failed, but your preparation was low, you experienced what is called inflated confidence. We can fall into that trap when we have outperformed others consistently, have highly competent skillsets that haven't been tested against a course of fire or against other people's skillsets, or have not used multiple skillsets in complex situations. We also experience inflated confidence when we've been performing at a high level over a period of time and start to take the preparation variable for granted. To avoid falling victim to either false or inflated confidence, train in a systematic manner that negates the risk of not feeling confident and promotes effective strategies for achieving a consistent and high-level performance.

Many people tend to see a situation as the glass either being half full or half empty. To perform well, see the situation simply as a glass that holds something. By seeing it as value neutral, a concept introduced at the beginning of this chapter, we can begin to train our performance objectively. All other mental preparation and goal-setting methods are dependent on us putting the focus where it matters and ultimately on "What's Important Now." (Remember, repeatable processes produce predictable results!) Breaking these methods down and focusing on the different aspects of preparation, practice, and performance can seem daunting, but once we do, we start to make measurable progress. Then we can prepare for, and ultimately succeed in, almost any encounter we may face.

7 HOW TO BUILD A TRAINING PROGRAM

There are several approaches to training. Ask a good shooter, and they'll give you a specific plan. Find another one, and they'll give you a different but still specific training plan. Two different plans—same result. The fact that two different shooters can train differently and still get the same results should tell us a few things. First, it should tell us that individual approaches usually work best. The concept is known as "individual differences," and it means that we all perceive things differently, we all have different strengths and weaknesses, and we all learn and process information in a unique way. That's why different plans work for different people. Second, it should tell us that if we break training plans down, we should find some common elements in the way plans are built—which is why different people using different plans can get similar results. Therefore, we should direct our attention to the elements of effective training design, then find a way to make them work for us. I am not going to advocate for a specific plan for training to become a better pistol shooter. Instead, I'll discuss the elements of what makes a good training plan and outline a few strategies for putting them into action.

Before we get into the structures of practice, it is important that we talk about the manner in which we approach practice. K. Anders Ericsson is widely considered the leader of the field of study focused on the development of expertise. According to his volume of publications, the most fundamental approach to developing expertise includes a few main variables. The primary component is intention. We should be very intentional regarding our training. To do this, we should have very clear and specific goals or objectives for each training session we design for ourselves. What this means is that shooting one hundred intentional rounds can be much better training than going to the range and shooting one thousand mindless rounds. In both cases, we may improve, but if we can be intentional about our training, our improvement will be more significant, and we will retain more of that improvement. The other aspect of our approach, as influenced by Ericsson, is being deliberate. Essentially, it means that we'll start with a goal, build a plan to meet it, monitor our progress, and make changes as needed based on the feedback we get from training.

TYPES OF FEEDBACK

There are three basic types of feedback we get when we do anything. The easiest one to notice is referred to as "task intrinsic feedback." Task intrinsic feedback includes the way our movement patterns feel (called proprioception) and the other sensory feedback we get as we perform the task—like what we see, hear, and smell. The best example of task intrinsic feedback when learning to shoot a pistol is often the grip. As already discussed, the grip is a three-piece jigsaw puzzle comprised of the pistol, our shooting hand, and our support hand. Our job is to put our puzzle together in a way that best receives the physics of recoil. In order to do that, we have to be aware of how the gun feels in our hands when we draw it, when the trigger is pressed, and immediately after the trigger is pressed. All the information you gain from your senses while you present and fire the gun is task intrinsic. Because our senses are something that only we can experience, we need two more types of feedback to confirm our process is effective.

The most objective type of feedback is known as "knowledge of results" feedback. Knowledge of results (or KR) feedback tells us if we were successful in terms of the outcome. The desired outcome, of course, varies depending on our training plan and our approach to training. Since one of the common goals of shooting is to hit what we are aiming at, KR feedback can be as simple as a hit or a miss. If we are dry firing, the result we are looking for might be tracking our sight picture to make sure our sight alignment isn't disrupted when the trigger breaks. KR feedback is an important part of our development as shooters, but it doesn't always tell us the whole story. We know that we can hold the pistol in a variety of different manners and still get the bullet to hit the target, but just because we hit the target doesn't mean we are practicing a repeatable and predictable process. Therefore, just because we can get the outcome we want—a hit—without ensuring that what we did with the gun was the best, the most consistent, or the most repeatable way to get that bullet on target, it should also tell us that we need one last type of feedback to make sure that we are executing the skills that create consistent hits.

Knowledge of performance (or KP) feedback meets that need. This is external information, or critique, given to you through coaching or video replay. Getting this feedback can be more difficult for a few different reasons. The first difficulty is that it's really hard to be focused on what we're doing and on how well we are executing the process simultaneously. Knowledge of performance feedback is usually the source of and the solution to our frustrations on the range. The classic pistol example is when a right-handed shooter is consistently missing left on paper. He can't feel it; his shot feels normal. He can't see it; it looks like his sight alignment is solid. Knowledge of results only tells him that he's missing and leaving him with no answers. Knowledge of performance feedback is what he needs.

There are a few sources of KP feedback. The easiest is to get it from a training partner. Tell them your goal so they know what to look for, then ask them to watch you and tell you what you did. When you see where your bullet hit (KR feedback), partnered with what your partner told you they saw you do (KP feedback), you'll have a better idea of two things. First, you'll learn what is actually happening in your hands. Second, and most importantly, you can start to connect what you did with the gun to your results. When you can do this, you're beginning to gain mastery of shooting.

Most of the drills you'll find in this book pair KR and KP feedback. Each one focuses on the performance aspect more than the result of the drill, and now you know why. When you get to the point where you understand that your results (e.g., bullet impacts) are a reflection of your performance (e.g., what happened in your hands), you can start to coach yourself. It's a signal that you are gaining the knowledge necessary to become a better shooter. Self-evaluate what you sensed, compare it to your performance information, and confirm it with your result information.

THE THREE-STAGE MODEL OF LEARNING

To consistently become better shooters, we should understand there's a learning curve in place. While many different theories of learning have been postulated, the Fitts and Posner three-stage model of skill acquisition seems to apply most readily to the majority of people training with weapons. The three stages, in order, are the cognitive, associative, and autonomous stages of learning.

The cognitive stage is where the shooter is gaining an understanding of basic movements and goals for training. In this stage, the cognitive load is generated by the amount of feedback needed to learn the movement patterns and goal structures. We are trying to understand where our shooting hand should be in relation to our support hand (and feet and eyes, for that matter), how timing and space impact shooting, what our goals should be, and how we should measure them. In this stage, mistakes are common and significant, which limits consistency and awareness. We are inconsistent because we are still learning our fundamentals—we can't yet repeat any of them. It makes sense, then, that our errors are frequent and significant as we continue the process of trying to perform a skill, evaluating our performance, making an adjustment, trying it again, reevaluating, and so on, either until we are so frustrated that we quit, or so motivated that we figure it out. It is important to cut ourselves some slack in the cognitive stage, as permitting ourselves to make some mistakes lessens self-critical judgment and promotes the adjustment-seeking mindset crucial to being development-focused.

The associative stage is where the shooter has learned to associate specific environmental cues with the movements needed to achieve the goal of the practice session, drill, competition stage, or combat application. Because there is no specified amount or duration of practice, or any kind of performance indicators marking the transition between the cognitive and associative phases of learning, it's up to the shooter to train the fundamentals with intention and according to his individual preferences. The resulting knowledge is generated by the ability to relate the elements of shooting with the elements of practice.

The last stage is termed the autonomous stage and is ultimately the goal of everyone who has ever tried to master anything. The autonomous stage is characterized by three main effects. First, the movements and the decision to engage those movements have become automated in a way that requires very little to no conscious thought. The second characterization of this stage is marked by an ability to successfully execute a shooting skillset while doing something else—for example, firing an accurate shot while moving or while shooting from an unconventional shooting position behind cover—which makes shooting a useable skillset. The third characterization is that shooters who have accomplished this level of learning are capable of noticing their mistakes and choosing adjustments that lead to consistent and improved results. Because of the amount of effort it takes to successfully execute these conditions, not everyone will make it to this stage of learning. Despite this, understanding the system of learning allows us to introduce and utilize macro and micro cycles (more on this in a minute) in our training and maintain a development-focused mindset throughout our training iterations.

When we take into account individual differences, the types and uses of feedback, and the three-stage learning cycle, we can design a training program that both employs the most common elements of human performance and learning and also specifically targets those skillsets we most need to improve. The best designs layer micro cycles of isolated fundamentals under macro cycles of combined fundamentals—essentially, practicing the cognitive stage specifically for setting up the associative stage—as we learn to associate fundamentals with our larger training goals until they become automated. Reaching this level of training is a significant achievement since once you reach the autonomous stage in one specific fundamental, you can then continuously add to it by layering another cycle of a different fundamental over it. Before we do any of that, though, we need to determine our shooting goals.

GOALS REVISITED

We can't be intentional and deliberate without goals. All practice design strategies are determined by our goals, and only you can set your goals. Are you a recreational shooter or someone who carries a weapon for their job? The answer to that question will inform the motivation behind your goals.

Recreational shooters want to learn to shoot because it's fun. Generally, the recreational shooter's goals are fundamental accuracy and basic weapon handling proficiency. People generally don't enjoy things they are bad at, so if you're out to have fun and enjoy shooting, it makes sense that you'd be interested in hitting what you're aiming at. Hobbyists are next-level recreational shooters. The hobbyist is someone who will shoot mostly for recreation but who will also enjoy shooting in local competitions. The hobbyist's goals will be slightly more complex than the recreational shooter's, as they're bound to include more performance-based goals focused on weapon manipulations and movement.

We can also talk about competition shooters' goals. The competition shooter will still need accuracy goals, but also speed, firing rate, manipulations, and movement goals. The competition shooter's goals will need to be more precise and performance-based than either the recreational shooter or the hobbyist, and as a result, they are more complex yet. At the same time, the competition shooter shares one very important goal in common with the recreational shooter and the hobbyist: all three need to develop their skills and their proficiency at executing those skills in order to know and be in control of the conditions and standards under which they will fire their weapons. Even high-level competition shooters get to walk through a stage and make a performance plan before shooting the stage.

The last general category of shooters includes those who carry a weapon as a term of their employment—police, military, and law enforcement agencies. I'll refer to them as the professional group of shooters because the outcomes of their firearms engagement have literal life-or-death consequences. Their training goals are more difficult to determine because the environmental contexts in which they may have to employ their weapons are always reactionary and never predetermined. Even in a high-level military raid, when the shooters know they will have to fire their weapons, they have no way of knowing when or at what. Consequently, this general group of shooters lacks an established set of performance metrics for guaranteeing success. Whereas the other three categories of shooters definitively know what it would take to satisfy their competency expectations, the professional group is only evaluated on the results of the mission requirements. Because of this, they generally focus on reaching the autonomous stage of shooting fundamentals so they can use their remaining attentional bandwidth for decision-making in dynamic, high-consequence environments.

Because the range of goals that shooters may have varies greatly, it makes sense to learn the most common elements of practice design, which can then be applied to your specific shooting goals.

ELEMENTS OF PRACTICE DESIGN

The basic purpose of practice is to improve. In other words, what we practice and the way we practice it should transfer to our performance goals. Transfer is a function of the similarity between skills, context, and cognition of practice and performance conditions. The more similar our practice conditions are to our performance goals, the more effective our practice becomes. All practice design, therefore, should start with skills development, then focus on context before adding in cognition.

The first stage in the progression of skill development is to learn the fundamentals, or tasks, involved in a given skill. Mastery of these various tasks becomes our process goal. Once we've mastered each task within a skill, we put them together to see how well we can execute the skill using either accuracy (how well we did the skill) or speed (how fast we completed the skill) as a measure of our success. This information will then determine our performance goals. Skills development informs process and performance goals; context and cognition (knowing when and how to use said skills) inform outcome goals.

For example, if we are learning to do a slide lock reload, then the process goal is to get ten straight perfectly executed slide lock reloads. Once we can do that, we time it to see how long it took us. That time establishes a baseline performance goal, which we can then test in whatever context we plan to use the skill or anytime there are other environmental factors dividing our attention. After that, we can set an outcome goal to improve our time or accuracy. All we have to do is revisit our process, break it back down to make adjustments, and repeat the cycle.

To develop fundamental skills, we need to approach our practice with limited variability at first, then progressively add variability. Practice variability means practicing several variations of a skill, whereas constant practice refers to practicing only one variation of a skill. Including more variability in our practice will produce more errors in practice; however, it also produces better skill retention and transfers to our performance goals. There are many ways to add or subtract variability into our shooting practice, and the way the drills are laid out in this book will help you do it. You can also create your own drills and add or subtract variability as needed.

When it comes to adding or subtracting variability in practice, we first need to consider which conditions are variable. The science of motor control uses the terms "regulatory and nonregulatory conditions" to describe the ways a practice session can be influenced. Regulatory conditions are the characteristics or features of the environmental context that influence which movement characteristics we need to perform. They are not themselves the movement, only the environment *regulating* the movement needed—thus, regulatory conditions. Nonregulatory conditions of the performance environment, as the name suggests, do not influence the movement needed to perform.

Here's an example. If I ask you to shoot three ten-round iterations, each at an eight-inch target located ten meters away, and tell you that for the first iteration, you will have thirty seconds, the next only twenty, and the last only ten, then the variable regulatory condition is the time allotted to shoot ten rounds. I've observed thousands of Special Forces operators shoot that exact drill and can tell you that the vast majority of the time, the ten-second iteration has more bullets in the target than the other two iterations. Here's the reason: the ten-second iteration only allows enough time to think about the three things that make bullets hit targets—grip, sight picture, and trigger squeeze. In the other iterations, they have time to evaluate their performance, make adjustments to their sight pictures, and judge themselves. What they learn from that drill is to separate out the conditions. If you can shoot ten rounds in the target in ten seconds, you can certainly do it in double and triple that time. Therefore, if you struggled with the first two iterations, either you don't understand the fundamentals of shooting, or you can't separate out the conditions that influenced your movements.

When we think of pistol shooting, we should think about the factors that are always constant and those that are not. Generally, the fundamentals of grip, sight picture, and trigger press will be constant, regardless of the conditions. Factors like speed, target size, and movement do change, which means that they can be used to add variability to your practice design. So can cognitive load (generated by pairing different types of feedback) and stacking fundamentals. Now let's start putting things together.

PRACTICE SCHEDULES

There are three fundamental practice schedules. Blocked practice is when the same skill is practiced for the whole session. Blocked practice has the least variability and highest consistency, making it a sound strategy for learning a new skill, retraining a skill that has become deficient, or altering a previously learned skill. While using a blocked practice schedule can be very effective, there are some reasons why we don't want to do too much of it. The primary reason is that it doesn't provide enough of what is called "contextual interference" in our practice sessions. Contextual interference pushes us beyond the cognitive stage and into the associative stage of learning. We need memory and performance environment disruptions to learn and grow. Additionally, one of the common outcomes of blocked practice is a consistent overestimation of what has been learned. Overestimating our capabilities is dangerous because it limits our development as shooters and also undermines our performances.

Serial practice schedules rotate skills in a predetermined order during practice sessions. For instance, if your training goal was to improve your concealed carry draw, then you could draw from the appendix position, then the four o'clock position, then OWB (outside the waistband) with a sport coat. Then you would repeat that order, in the same order, to make it a serial schedule. Using a serial schedule provides you with more contextual interference than blocked practice schedules and can be used as a sound method of stacking fundamentals for skill development or mixing techniques to better replicate the performance environment.

Random practice schedules provide the most contextual interference and therefore the highest error rates in practice conditions. If you were to use a random schedule to practice the same concealed carry draw positions, you would do the same number of repetitions or practice for the same amount of time, but you would randomize the order of the skills. Instead of working progressively around the clock, you could start with OWB four o'clock, then appendix, then IWB four o'clock, then appendix, then IWB four o'clock, then OWB four o'clock. Random practice schedules help you to develop more strategies, and more strategies, in turn, promote more elaborate memory representations of the skill. Memory (or mental) representations of skills are a defining characteristic of expertise and lead the way to skill mastery.

AMOUNT OF CONTEXTUAL INTERFERENCE

Figure 7.1

High		Low
Random Schedule	Serial Schedule	Blocked Schedule

PRACTICE SCHEDULE

Before we continue into the specifics of designing training programs, we need to discuss some limiting factors of the fundamentals. First, we need to reiterate the limits of increasing contextual interference. If we choose to combine different skills, then our contextual interference effect will be less than if we choose to combine variations of similar skills. For example, if we set a goal to work on breaking the shot as we reach full presentation and built a random practice schedule focusing on the skills of the draw, the sight alignment, and shooting in cadence, the contextual interference would be low. There's not a common factor related to our goal among those skills. If, however, we built one using a press out, a draw, and a depressed muzzle position, then the contextual interference would be high because we need to time the trigger break with a full presentation in three different ways to get to full presentation.

Figure 7.2

DRAWS							
BLOCKED	30 mins	Sides	Sides	Up	Up	Turn	Turn
SERIAL	5 mins	Sides	Sides	Sides	Sides	Sides	Sides
	5 mins	Up	Up	Up	Up	Up	Up
	5 mins	Turn	Turn	Turn	Turn	Turn	Turn
	5 mins	Sides	Sides	Sides	Sides	Sides	Sides
	5 mins	Up	Up	Up	Up	Up	Up
	5 mins	Turn	Turn	Turn	Turn	Turn	Turn
RANDOM	5 mins	Sides	Sides	Turn	Sides	Up	Turn
	5 mins	Up	Turn	Sides	Turn	Sides	Sides
	5 mins	Sides	Turn	Turn	Turn	Up	Turn
	5 mins	Turn	Up	Up	Up	Turn	Up
	5 mins	Sides	Sides	Up	Sides	Up	Up
	5 mins	Up	Sides	Turn	Sides	Sides	Turn

Finally, in regard to practice schedules, it's important to reiterate that higher contextual interference from random practice leads to more frequent errors in practice, higher strategy generation, higher attentional demand, better mental representations, better transfer, better estimation of competency expectations in performance, and therefore, better retention from practice to performance. Lower contextual interference from blocked practice leads to less frequent practice errors, lower strategy development, less attentional demand, less complex mental representations, less transfer, an overestimation of competency expectations, and less retention from practice to performance. When we are new to a skill, we should start with blocked practice and follow the continuum in Figure 7.1 to promote development.

FURTHER PRACTICE DESIGN FACTORS

Now that we have the building blocks of developing practice, we need to understand a few defining factors of motor skill learning and performance to really hone our practice sessions. We'll start with the three common characteristics of skill learning, move to some guidelines regarding how we break down the skills, then discuss the frequency and duration of practice and the common outcomes of those strategies.

Most of the information we learn about our environment comes from our vision, especially as our skills are developing. What that tells us is that we first need to know what to look at, what to look for, and how to connect what we see to our goals. A simple example would be a right-handed shooter missing to the left. We see the sight alignment is good, but we also see the bullet impact to the left, which tells us that something in our grip or trigger press is causing the impact to miss the mark. Another example would be watching someone demonstrate a movement, then trying to replicate the movement. For instance, we watch a video in which a shooter draws his pistol and shoots, and then we try to replicate the movement on our own.

At first, the visual feedback is really important, but as our skills develop, the proprioceptive (or the feel of the movement) feedback becomes a more significant source of information. Once we develop a repeatable grip with a predictable bullet impact, we don't need to see the bullet's impact to know where the bullet hit the target, commonly known as "calling your shot." We can feel that the grip was off and know that the bullet will follow. At the same time, because we gain most of our sensory input from our visual system, we should be aware that our vision will dominate our feedback cycles, making it harder to focus on the feel of the movement. This is one reason why practice conditions with high contextual interference create higher frequency errors in practice. You'll miss more, but you'll learn more, and the things you learn will stick with you longer.

The second defining factor in skill learning is that the environment you learn in can give you cues, sometimes unintended cues, that feed your ability to execute the skill. While these cues can be beneficial for learning, they can be detrimental for performance. Therefore, we need to balance this factor as we practice and use it as a way to adjust variability—and by extension, contextual interference—in our practice. An easy example is a mirror in front of a squat rack in a weight room. If you use the mirror to determine when your thighs are parallel to the ground, you'll be able to replicate this depth mark relatively easily. However, if you never squat without the mirror, or if you never direct your attention to the proprioceptive cues your body gives you regarding depth, you'll struggle to execute that squat depth without the aid of the mirror. In shooting, a simple example of your environment offering you cues would be shooting paper IPSC-style targets in practice, then shooting cardboard IPSC targets in competition. Most paper targets use different colors for each scoring zone, whereas the cardboard targets are either completely brown or white. If you practice with the color paper targets, you'll learn to use the contrasting colors to align your sights, even if you aren't instructed to do so or don't intend to, and then in competition, your accuracy will be degraded. The lesson in what is referred to as "performance context" characteristics is that you will learn more about the context than you are instructed to learn or intend to learn. The performance context characteristics are the source of common sayings such as "Train like you fight."

The last common characteristic has to do with the amount of information you need to process in order to meet the demands of the transfer goal. This is another reason why goals are so important in our training. Regardless of complexity or cognitive load, our practice sessions should incorporate the same amount of cognitive processing needed in our performance goal. When we practice, one of the things we learn is how much mental effort will be necessary to do whatever it is we are practicing. If you're practicing for something that is mentally demanding, then your practice should be equally mentally demanding. The "cognitive processing" characteristic of learning a skill is also a sound manner to determine your competency expectations. If you're overloaded as you stack fundamentals or combine skillsets, then you can make a reasonable estimation of what you're capable of in a performance setting.

Using these three common characteristics helps us determine how to build practice sessions based on our development and regardless of our performance goals. First, we need to determine the complexity of the skill. Fundamentals are the least complex skills, but as we stack them together, they become more complex. For instance, if we were to shoot the Cadence Drill, we would be stacking several fundamentals—grip, sight picture, and trigger press—into a skill development practice. Note that we've already stacked grip and sight picture for sight alignment, and in order to shoot multiple targets in cadence, we also have to stack trigger press and trigger reset. At the same time, we are stacking our vision fundamentals of sight and target focus, as well as our shooting fundamentals of stance and grip for managing recoil. The complexity assessment is dependent on our current ability.

The next thing we need to consider is skill organization, or how the parts of our skill are related to each other. We already know that grip is related to sight alignment, recoil management, and focal shift for our vision, and those three combined create sight picture. We also already know that trigger press and trigger reset are related. The aspect we are practicing is combining these skills together as we move from target to target so that our shots sound like a metronome. The goal of the drill is to reinforce those stacked fundamentals and add the skill of reducing the time it takes to transition from one target to the next. Once we understand the complexity and organization of the drill, we are practicing in terms of the performance goal, which means we can better diagnose our deficiencies while enhancing our intention and deliberation in our practice.

STRATEGIES FOR ALTERING TASK DIFFICULTIES

There are five basic strategies for altering task difficulties. The particular order presented here is not reflective of their importance to you and your practice. Once you have a training goal and an understanding of your competency when executing fundamentals, you'll be able to determine which of the five basic strategies to use for the purposes of increasing or decreasing the difficulty of the task.

One strategy is to alter the object, which means you could use bigger targets to make shooting less difficult or smaller targets to make it more difficult. You could move the targets closer to make shooting easier or further away to make it harder. You could change your sights. You could use a gun that fits your hands better. The list goes on—what you alter will depend on your specific practice and performance goals.

Another strategy you could use is to alter the attentional demands. If you want to make shooting harder, add more contextual interference—things like more movement, no-shoot targets, colored targets, reactive targets, or a smaller sight. If you wanted to make it easier, you could reduce the number of things you have to think about while you're shooting.

A third strategy is to change your shooting speed. Reducing the speed will help with coordination and retention; increasing the speed will make it more difficult to execute the skill. A fourth strategy would be to add auditory cues—generally, internal cue words—to the skill to make it easier. Common examples include telling yourself, "Sight, slack, squeeze," to learn the fundamental trigger press, or counting cadences in your head as you shoot a half-count cadence: "One and two and..." When you take these auditory cues away, it becomes more difficult to repeat a performance.

Finally, the most fundamental strategy for altering task difficulty is simply to adjust the complexity. Build progressions by adding steps to your skill organization to increase complexity. To make a skill easier, remove a few steps.

FREQUENCY AND DURATION OF PRACTICE SESSIONS

Lastly, we need to consider the frequency and duration of practice sessions. In terms of transfer and retention, we should work toward having higher frequency, lower duration practices. Considering your goals, practice schedule options, and the specific factors of practice will determine how much you can reasonably expect to accomplish in the time you have to practice. Another consideration is intensity. From a practice perspective, intensity will be a subjective assessment of cognitive load. Because of the importance of intentional practice and focus, your practice quality will deteriorate as a function of the attentional demand required to complete it. Therefore, when planning a practice session, you can use the relative intensity of skills as markers to break up skills when planning serial or random practice schedules by adding a blocked practice session in the middle or by simply taking a break.

Some additional considerations when determining frequency and duration of practice include perceptions of learning and practical applications. Perceptions of learning are an effect of practice design. We've already established that people who complete blocked practice routines consistently overestimate their abilities, while people who complete random practice routines consistently have more errors in their practice sessions. To avoid these higher error rates, most people opt for longer but less frequent practice sessions over a shorter time in a blocked schedule than more frequent, shorter practice sessions over a longer time in a random schedule. Doing so makes you look better on paper but won't help you as much long term. If you want to stick to your long-term goals, try practicing more often using a randomized skills schedule. Also, remember that it's okay to just have fun sometimes in practice!

Ultimately, your practice design will also be the result of lifestyle factors like access to ranges, ammunition budgets, targets, and time to practice. It's not always realistic to go to the range on a high-frequency, low-duration schedule, even if it is the best way to practice. We can still use common sense and practicality when designing practice schedules. If you can only make it to the range once a week, divide up the time into sessions. If you only have one hundred rounds, divide them up into random skills practices. Practice design allows you to assess what resources you have and make the best of them as you work toward your goals. There are very few hard and fast rules; instead, take what time, ammo, and space you have and put it to work for you in the most effective way possible.

APPENDIX I
EXAMPLE TRAINING PROGRAMS

HOW TO USE THE TRAINING PLAN

BAER SOLUTIONS

Focus your efforts. Pick something to deliberately work on and improve.

Don't waste rounds being a cold shooter. Get your body and mind warmed up with some movement and visualization.

Pick an Evaluation type drill or CTE that matches the skill(s) you are focusing on to see where you're at and get the day off with a goal.

After the Cold Start, focus on mastering the fundamentals. Think about being an expert, get really good at these. Make some notes about what right feel feels like.

Now that you know where you stand with a skill and you've tuned the fundamentals, the work begins. Build a list of drills, set a goal to be better than you were when you started. Now it's time to push the speed and/or accuracy. Do it systematically. Small, incremental improvements.

Now that you've tuned the fundamentals, and practiced the skills, it's time to see what you can do. The outcome goal is to see what you can do—not to push what you've already done.

GROUP 1 – MECHANICS				
PRE WORKOUT				
Finger/Forearm Exercise, Strengthening, Stretching				
COLD START				
BAER Standards	Time		Notes	
El Prez	Time		Notes	
SKILL (PROCESS FOCUSED)				
	Focus Point 1	Focus Point 2	Focus Point 3	Notes
Full Draw				
Reloads				
L and R Transitions				

APPLICATION (PERFORMANCE FOCUSED)						
	GOAL	Rep 1	Rep 2	Rep 3	Rep 4	Notes
Full Draw						
Reloads						
Draw, reload on different tgt/spot						
Reloads, moving						
Transitions, Wide						
Transition, Near						
Throttle Control, HP/LP Targets						

EVALUATION (OUTCOME FOCUSED)						
	GOAL	Rep 1	Rep 2	Rep 3	Rep 4	Notes
"BILL DRILL"						
"El Prez"						

POST WORKOUT
Finger/Forearm Exercise, Strengthening, Stretching Equipment Maintenance

Example 1

GROUP 1 – MECHANICS					

PRE WORKOUT					

Finger/Forearm Exercise, Strengthening, Stretching

COLD START					
BAER Standards	Time		Notes		
El Prez	Time		Notes		

SKILL (PROCESS FOCUSED)

	Focus Point 1	Focus Point 2	Focus Point 3	Notes
Full Draw				
Reloads				
L and R Transitions				

APPLICATION (PERFORMANCE FOCUSED)

	GOAL	Rep 1	Rep 2	Rep 3	Rep 4	Notes
Full Draw						
Reloads						
Draw, reload on different tgt/spot						
Reloads, moving						
Transitions, Wide						
Transition, Near						
Throttle Control, HP/LP Targets						

EVALUATION (OUTCOME FOCUSED)

	GOAL	Rep 1	Rep 2	Rep 3	Rep 4	Notes
"BILL DRILL"						
"El Prez"						

POST WORKOUT

Finger/Forearm Exercise, Strengthening, Stretching
Equipment Maintenance

Example 2

GROUP 2 - PRESENTATIONS

PRE WORKOUT

Finger/Forearm Exercise, Strengthening, Stretching

COLD START				
BAER Standards	Time		Notes	
Dawson 100	Time		Notes	

SKILL (PROCESS FOCUSED)

	Time	PSA x	Notes	
5 by Trigger ISO				
2rd Strings				
3rd Strings				

APPLICATION (PERFORMANCE FOCUSED)

	GOAL	Rep 1	Rep 2	Rep 3	Rep 4	Notes
High Ready						
Low Ready						
HOG Draw						
Full Draw						
Draw, Hands Up						
Draw, Turns, F/L/R/B						
Draw, 3 Step, F/L/R/B						
Draw, Moving F/L/R/B						

EVALUATION (OUTCOME FOCUSED)

	GOAL	Rep 1	Rep 2	Rep 3	Rep 4	Notes
"BILL DRILL"						
Dawson 100						

POST WORKOUT

Finger/Forearm Exercise, Strengthening, Stretching

Equipment Maintenance

Example 3

GROUP 3 - MOVEMENT

PRE WORKOUT

Finger/Forearm Exercise, Strengthening, Stretching

COLD START

BAER Standards	Time		Notes	
HP/LP CTE	Time		Notes	

SKILL (PROCESS FOCUSED)

	Time	PSA x	Notes	
High Ready/Low Ready				
Draws				
Reloads				

APPLICATION (PERFORMANCE FOCUSED)

	GOAL	Rep 1	Rep 2	Rep 3	Rep 4	Notes
M VMT, Static - to - Static						
M VMT, Short/Med/Long						
M VMT, Depth						
M VMT, Width						
M VMT, L Drill						
M VMT, HP and LP tgts						
M VMT, HP and LP tgts						

EVALUATION (OUTCOME FOCUSED)

	GOAL	Rep 1	Rep 2	Rep 3	Rep 4	Notes
Practice Stage 1						
Practice Stage 2						

POST WORKOUT

Finger/Forearm Exercise, Strengthening, Stretching
Equipment Maintenance

APPENDIX II
DRILLS

Task/Skills

- Trigger Iso
- Recoil Management
- Now Drill
- Seth's Rhythm Drills
- Distance Marksmanship

Context/Application

- Low Ready
- High Ready
- HOG Draw
- Full Draw
- Tac Mag/Combat Reloads
- Reload Malfunction
- 3-Step Draw

- Cadence at Distance
- Multitarget Transitions
- Throttle Control
- El Prez 2.0

Creative/Evaluation
- BAER Through It
- Target ID
- BAER Standard
- Dawson 100
- Dawson 100 2.0

SLACK, SIGHT, PRESS

WHAT

Fire one round at a time at the 1" circle/paster with firing hand for an entire magazine. Then do the same with the non-firing hand, firing hand again, and lastly with both hands.

WHY

At its most basic, only two things are required to put an accurate round on target. Sights aligned and trigger straight to the rear. The best shooters in the world don't look for where their shot hit, they know where it hit because they **saw** the sights aligned properly and **felt** the trigger pull was correct. To know what a good shot is you have to know what a bad shot is. The purpose of this drill is to establish that. We do it with both hands so that you can feel all the minor imperfections in your non-firing hand, which will translate to the firing hand.

Most people think they are pulling the trigger straight back, but the shot group says otherwise. If your finger is pulling into open space, then you have no reference for what straight is. To establish this you need to have a reference point. With an unloaded gun hold the pistol out with only your firing hand. Dryfire the gun so that you are pulling the trigger to the four different angles. **Elbow, wrist, thumb knuckle**, and **thumb tip**. You should see the trigger pull affect the sights differently with each different angle. Identify which one keeps the sights on target the best, and at most causes the sights to "vibrate" over the target. Where your finger touches the trigger shoe is different for everyone. Don't use the tip, pad or knuckle is good for most. Remember, everyone has different sized hands and levers, so smaller hands with shorter digits will mean an angle pulling more to the outside than larger hands with longer digits.

HOW

Start with the gun on target, slack out of trigger and break each shot individually for the entire mag. Once complete, move onto next step.
With this drill you can't gauge the progress or "success" of the shooter by looking at the target. We're not as concerned with the shot group as we are with the bullet going where the sights were

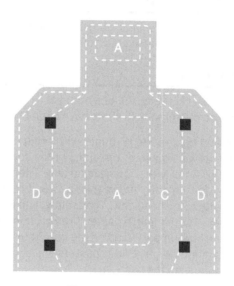

1" pasters at 3m

Method	Rounds
Firing Hand	15
Support Hand	15
Firing Hand	15
Both Hands	15

indexed. If the bullet goes where the sights were, great. If not, then we need to correct it. To correct we actually over correct. For example, if a right-handed shooter's sights were on the center of the target and the round impacted to the left, then that is most likely because the trigger pull direction was to the left instead of straight back. To correct this, dig your finger in the trigger, pull at a more extreme angle outside (i.e. outside of your elbow) and make the round impact to the right of the sights. You know what wrong left is, you know what wrong right is, now you cancel both out and can put one in the middle. The middle being where your sights are pointed.

CONCLUSION

This is a challenging drill and you may notice the shot group open up as you go between the different steps. That's fine. You will see the shot group tighten up when you put it all together with both hands.

START POSITION

Standing at the 3 m cone, facing down range, holding gun with sights on paster, gun fully loaded.

PROCEDURE

When shooter is ready, fire one round at a time at the designated paster until 15 shots have been fired.

For the first paster, fire 15 rounds with firing hand only. Then reload, and reset for the drill. For the second paster, fire 15rds with support hand only. Then reload and reset for the drill. For the third paster, fire 15 rounds with firing hand only. Then reload and reset for the drill. For the fourth paster, fire 15 rounds with both firing and support hand on the gun. Your firing hand will mimic your previous pasters and support hand is steadying the gun.

DO

- Make each shot count.
- Focus is on the process during your performance.
- Confirm the result after you bring the sights back on the paster.

FEEL

- Your contact point of the pad of your finger on the trigger and how it lines up as trigger pulls to reference point.
- The firing platform spreading the gun which locks the wrist.
- The thumb knuckle wrapping up around beaver tail toward target.

SEE

- Equal height and equal light on top of your sights.
- The sights lift straight up to call your shot.
- The sights return onto the paster mirroring sight picture before.
- The return as lift in reverse.

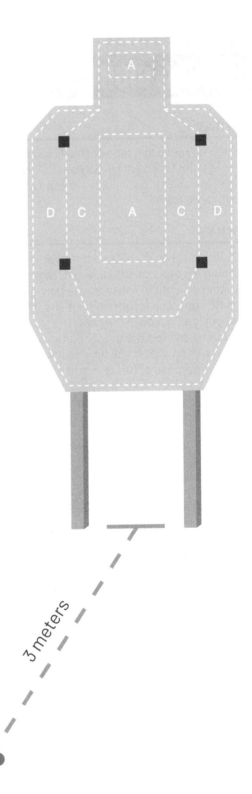

3 meters

SPREAD, TORQUE, WEDGE

WHAT

Starting with the pistol on target, fire 5 rounds at a comfortable pace applying the most recoil management needed to have the sights return to the same index point. Start easy and then pick up speed to fine tune the recoil management applied. You can start with a larger circle and then use smaller ones to test yourself.

WHY

Recoil management is one half of being "shooter ready" as JJ Racaza calls it. The trigger portion was addressed in the Now Drill. If each time you pull the trigger you know where the gun will return, or re-index to, then you can take the guess work out of your shots and trust your shooting more.

You goal here is to apply as much needed "from the start" so that each shot is the same. Whether it's the first or tenth shot, you have a repeatable process that will produce a predictable result. Locking the gun in is one less thing your brain has to think about so you can free up your bandwidth to solve problems in front of you and put focus in more important places.

HOW

First, build your grip on the firearm like we discussed earlier in the book. **Spread, torque, press.**

Second, set your vision. You need to be able to see the sights move in recoil to know what effect the recoil management you are applying is having on the gun through your shot string. If you are narrow target focused on the front sight it's a lot like seeing through a small window. As the gun goes off and through it's recoil, it will leave that window and then return without you being able to see where it went and what it did. Set your vision so that you see "everything". Don't focus on the target, don't focus on the sights, set your plane of focus somewhere in the middle so that you notice the surroundings with your peripherals.

Lastly, fire your five rounds and "notice" what the sights are doing in recoil. Are they going straight up, off to the left, off to the right, too high, nose dips

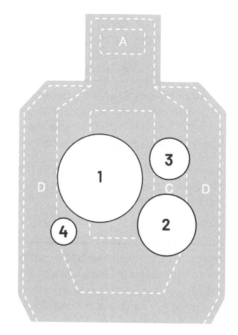

6" or 3" circles at 5 meters

Method	Rounds
Both Hands	5 round strings
Repeat for 9 strings	Total: 45

down, etc? This is your indicator of what you need to do here. As you shoot your 5 round strings, apply more recoil management as you go through it. Once you've identified what is ideal, do that from the start to the finish of the subsequent strings. Your first shot should be the same as the last. We don't build recoil management as you shoot, you establish it from the beginning.

CONCLUSION

Recoil management is not only about locking the gun so that sights lift and return in the same way. It's just as much about vision. See through your sights so that you can get feedback on what your sights are doing through recoil. See the lift so in the future you can call the shot. See the sights return so that you have good follow through.

START POSITION

Standing at the 5 m cone, facing down range, holding gun with sights on target, gun fully loaded.

PROCEDURE

Shooter holds sights on target with trigger at the wall, then shoots a 5 round string only as fast as you can see the sights lift and return to the same index point, and feel how you are framing out the pistol.

Improve each successive 5 round string so that your first shot is the same as 2nd, 3rd, 4th, and 5th. "It's about consistency Brian."

DO

- Reset the sights and trigger as fast as possible.
- Frame the pistol out so the sights return to the same spot.
- Shoot at a pace you can think and feel your way through.

FEEL

- Your firing platform and spreading of the gun.
- Your support hand torquing forward.
- Your elbows wedging the gun forward for the sights to realign naturally.

SEE

- Equal height and equal light on top of your sights.
- The sights lift straight up to call your shot.
- The sights return onto the paster mirroring sight picture before.
- The return as lift in reverse.

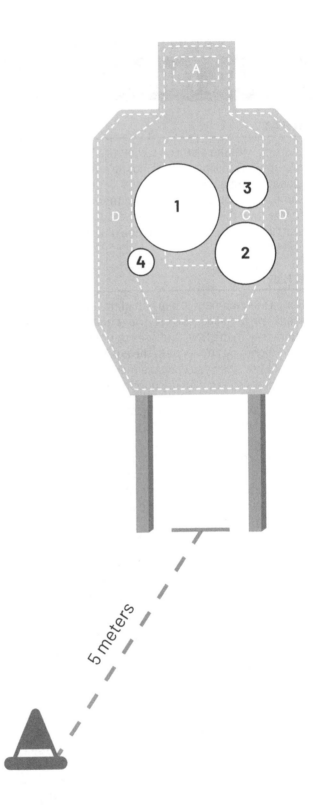

5 meters

PULLING THE TRIGGER IS A REACTION OF THE EYES SEEING THE SIGHTS ON TARGET.

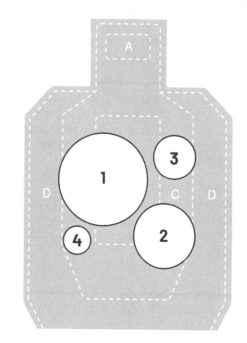

6" or 3" circles at 5 meters

Method	Rounds
Both Hands	15
Repeat for 3 mags	Total: 45

WHAT

Press gun onto target with sights aligned and slack taken out of the trigger. Partner taps shooter's shoulder to fire gun and shooter resets trigger back to wall as fast as possible. If done without a partner, then shooter tells themselves now and resets trigger as fast as possible back to wall.

WHY

The gun will always be ready faster than you. The key to speed while maintaining accuracy is to reset trigger and sights as fast as possible to be ready to shoot again, despite the size or distance of the target.

Having a partner tell you when to shoot takes the thinking out of shooting. The eyes seeing the sights aligned tells the finger to react. The finger doesn't tell the brain that the gun is about to go off. This is one place we get anticipation. This lets your partner do the thinking for you and you can focus on resetting the trigger, not pinning it, quicker to be shooter ready.

HOW

Start with perfect grip established, sights aligned on target and slack taken out of trigger so you can feel the wall. Partner standing off to the side so they can see the finger manipulate the trigger and hand ready to tap the shoulder to fire.

On start, partner taps the shooter to fire. When the trigger is reset back at wall, tap again. Vary the cadence to force fast reset and holding on the wall so that the shooter doesn't anticipate the "NOW" tap. Give feedback after 5-10 rounds or after each magazine.

Focus for shooter: reset trigger and sights back on target as fast as possible. Only react to the tap, do not think about pulling the trigger, think about resetting.

Focus for partner: watch the trigger, not the target. Don't randomly tap the shooter, tap him so that you can coach him to success.

CONCLUSION

If shooter is anticipating the tap, or pinning and slowly letting off, then vary the cadence. Speed them up to force a fast reset, then slow them down to hold at the wall for a more accurate shot. A double shot is not an ND here as long as the gun is pointed at the target. We are finding the wall of the trigger and it is bound to happen. Don't dwell on it, move on. Imagine the trigger finger has a rubber band attached to it and is being pulled back out after each shot.

START POSITION

Standing at the 5 m cone, facing down range, holding gun with sights on target, gun fully loaded.

PROCEDURE

Shooter holds sights on target with trigger at the wall, coach stands off to side able to see trigger manipulation. Coach calls standby when ready, then shooter reacts to the coach tapping them on the shoulder with firing one round.

Coach varies the count and taps to force shooter to vary shots between shooting faster and holding on the wall. Fire 15 rounds, or 1 magazine's worth of ammo. Repeat for a total of 3 magazines, then switch coach and shooter.

DO

- Reset the sights and trigger as fast as possible.
- React to the tap.
- Pull trigger to reference point you built on Trigger IsoDrill.

FEEL

- Your firing platform and spreading of the gun.
- Your support hand torquing forward.
- Your elbows wedging the gun forward for the sights to realign naturally.

SEE

- Equal height and equal light on top of your sights.
- The sights lift straight up to call your shot.
- The sights return onto the paster mirroring sight picture as before.
- The return as lift in reverse.

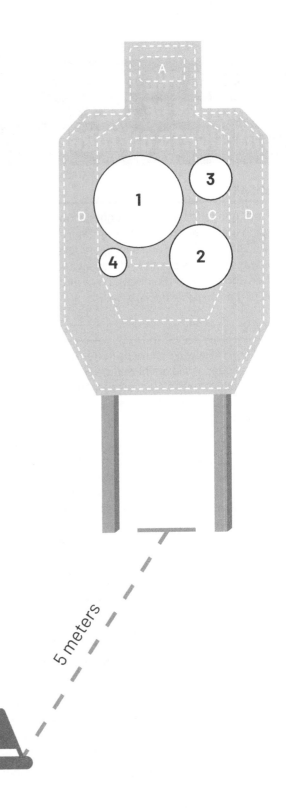

PULLING THE TRIGGER IS A REACTION OF THE EYES SEEING THE SIGHTS ON TARGET

PULLING THE TRIGGER IS A REACTION OF THE EYES SEEING THE SIGHTS ON TARGET

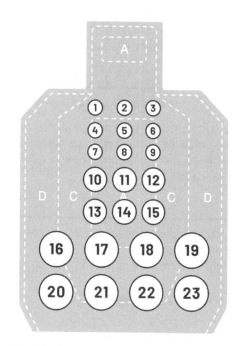

Seth's rhythm target at 5-10 meters

WHAT

Start with gun on target, holstered, or at a ready position, then engage the targets in the order prescribed in each progression listed. If this drill is tough for you, then start with gun on target. If easier, then add in a ready position or draw to each string.

WHY

Using rhythm drills are a great way to start to work on your vision and timing with each shot. Varying the size of the circles also begins to introduce throttle control. The better you can break your vision off of the current circle, once you have finished engaging that circle, the quicker you can identify the next target and engage.

Rhythm drills, like cadence drills, are often misunderstood. The reason we perform these is to be able to focus and see your sights during the engagement of each dot, and also to be able to do that while transitioning through multiple targets/dots. If we know how the gun will rise off target in recoil, and can trust that it will come back in the same place, then we can be confident as we transition the gun from target to target. The goal is to perform the strings of fire and be confident in trusting your sights to return to where you are looking, as well as trust your trigger pull.

HOW

Shift your focal plane back to confirm that the sights are aligned properly to achieve the level of accuracy needed to hit the different sized targets.

Follow the progression on the table below to build on your fundamentals. Focus on maintaining your cadences and seeing through the recoil to maintain sight picture. ON the progressions with more than one target, work to move your eyes to the next target first, then drive your sights. When you get to the last two progressions, work to maintain your cadence on the transitions between targets beginning the new cadence. Be safe, productive, and focused.

Method	Rounds
Both Hands	1-3 ea target
Repeat for 3 mags	Total: 45

Hammer Cadence: 3 meters | 12345 | "As fast as you can pull the trigger"

½ Cadence: 7 meters | 1,2,3,4,5, | "*bang, bang, bang...*"

¾ Cadence: 15 meters | 1, and 2, and 3, | "*bang and bang and bang...*"

Full Cadence: 25 meters | 1 thousand, 2 thousand, ... | "*bang*, thousand *bang*, thousand..."

CONCLUSION

Cadence drill can force you to be shooter ready faster, or give you extra time between shots to refine your sight picture for more accuracy. The faster you are shooter ready, sights back on target and trigger reset at the wall, the more time you have to use. Get comfortable shooting at faster cadences so you don't need as much time.

START POSITION

Standing at the 5 m cone, facing down range, holding gun with sights on target, gun fully loaded.

PROCEDURE

Upon start, draw and engage dots as prescribed.

Standard: No time limit, take only as much time as needed to finish the drill as fast as possible. Once you have a baseline, then incorporate time to achieve a standard and push yourself.

DO

- Reset the sights and trigger as fast as possible.
- Focus on the transition.
- Pull trigger to reference point you built on Trigger IsoDrill.
- Apply proper recoil management.

FEEL

- Yourself framing the gun out.
- The stippling against your support hand.
- The wall of the trigger with each shot.

SEE

- The next target and your sights align on it before you shoot.
- The lift and return on target or on the next target.

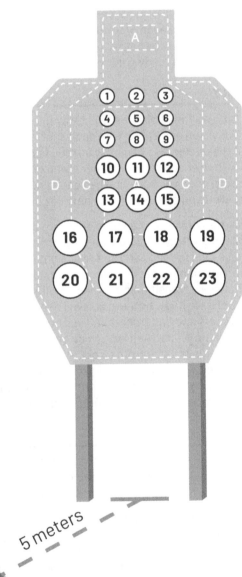

Progression	Cadence	Target Order	Rounds
1	Full	1, 1, 1, 1, 1	5
2	Full	1, 2, 3, 2, 1	5
3	Full	4, 4, 4, 4, 4	5
4	Full	4, 5, 6, 5, 4	5
5	Half	10, 10, 10, 10, 10	5
6	Half	10, 11, 12, 11, 10	5
7	Half	13, 13, 13, 13, 13	5
8	Half	13, 14, 15, 14, 13	5
9	Quarter	16, 16, 16, 16, 16	5
10	Quarter	16, 17, 18, 19, 18	5
11	Quarter	20, 20, 20, 20, 20	5
12	Quarter	20, 21, 22, 23, 22	5
13	Full	20	5
	Half	13	5
	Quarter	7	5
14	Quarter	9	5
	Half	15	5
	Full	23	5

5 meters

PULLING THE TRIGGER IS A REACTION OF THE EYES SEEING THE SIGHTS ON TARGET

TRUST THE SHOTS

WHAT

Start with gun on target or at a ready position, and engage the target (A zone, upper A zone, or 6" circle) with 5 rounds.

WHY

Trigger manipulation and recoil management doesn't change if we add distance or the target is smaller in relation to our sights. The only thing different is the time it takes to ensure our sights are properly aligned.

We all know this to be true but unfortunately, we don't do it. Instead shooters will usually perform unneeded actions like pinning the trigger, over exaggerating recoil, creeping the trigger, closing one eye, timing the shot off the release of the trigger, drawing the gun slow, presenting the gun slow, etc.

You need to reinforce this at distance because our brain tends to mess with our shooting as we add distance into the equation.

HOW

Start with perfect grip established, sights aligned on target and slack taken out of trigger so you can feel the wall. Shift your focal plane back to confirm that the sights are aligned properly to achieve the level of accuracy needed to hit the target at this distance.

Pull the trigger the same way you do at nearer distances (Slack, sight, press). Manage recoil the same way you do at nearer distances (Spread, torque, press). Here you can add in a focus point to confirm your sights more. Hands are **torquing** the frame, eyes confirm **sights**, and you **press** the trigger like in the now drill remembering your reference point from the trigger iso drill. Imagine what you see in front of you is just a 2D screen. There is no distance, just targets up on this screen of varying sizes. Shooting a 1" pasty at 3-5 meters is pretty similar to shooting the A zone at 25 meters. If the 1" pasty is easy, then this should be too.

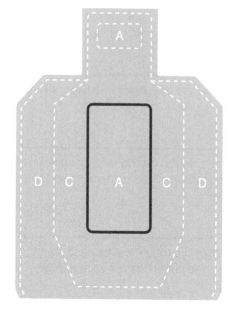

A Zone or ½ A Zone at 25 meters

Method	Rounds
Basic	5 in 10 seconds
Intermediate	5 in 7.5 seconds
Advanced	5 in 5 seconds

CONCLUSION

The key here is to make sure your shooting doesn't change at all, you just are taking the little bit extra time to confirm the sights are good enough. Holding on the wall for a split second before breaking the shot could be the difference in a good shot and a bad one.

START POSITION

Standing at the 25 m cone, facing down range, gun holstered or at ready position, gun fully loaded.

PROCEDURE

On start, engage the target with 5 rounds inside the A zone.

DO

- Reset the sights and trigger as fast as possible.
- Keep good form and avoid tensing up through the shot string.

FEEL

- The wall of the trigger before each shot.
- Framing the pistol through your elbows.

SEE

- Equal height and equal light on top of your sights.
- The sights lift straight up to call your shot.
- The sights return onto the paster mirroring sight picture before.
- The return is lift in reverse.

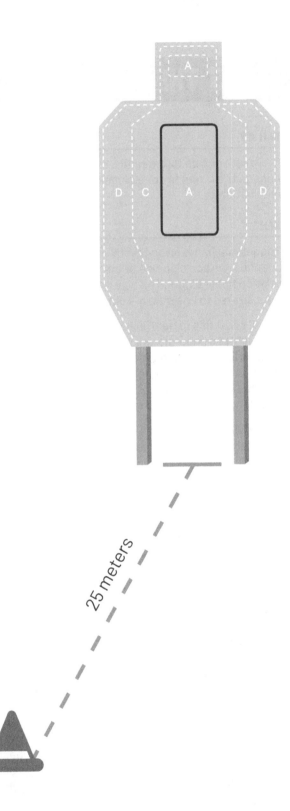

25 meters

UP, PREP, PRESS

WHAT

From hand *on* gun, engage a 6" circle with one round. Ensure you have proper follow through by resetting the trigger, and maintain recoil management so that the sights re-index back onto target.

WHY

You need to be ready to present your pistol from a multitude of positions. From the holster is definitely important, but you may have the gun out already before needing to take a shot. For a competition shooter, there is only one target on a stage, out of 10 or more, where you engage from the draw. For tactically or home defense minded shooters, you may have to respond to an incident or stimulus with the gun already out.

You can perform this two ways. Either arms at full presentation and raise the gun straight up, or with the gun broken back slightly so that it is partly a pressout and partly being raised up.

HOW

Start with gun pointed at a 45 degree angle toward the ground by either method mentioned above (arms straight or broken back toward the body). Relax your arms and shoulders.

On start, begin **raising/pressing the weapon** toward target and into your line of site while not moving anything but your arms. Begin to press your non-firing palm by **rotating it into the frame and "torquing"** it forward and down so that the thumb points forward. Body should be relaxed until the last portion where you lock the gun into place by applying your spread/torque on the gun.

As you are pressing the gun forward and up into your line of sight, place the finger on the trigger and take the slack out to the wall so that you are ready to break the **shot** as soon as the sights are aligned over the target.

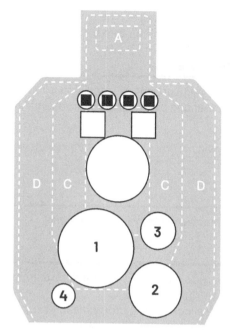

Circles or squares at 5-7 meters

Method	Rounds
Basic	1 in 1.5 seconds
Intermediate	1 in 1.25 seconds
Advanced	1 in 1.0 seconds
Progression: add rounds and distance	2+ at 7+ meters

Tie the motion of your hands meeting up and torquing into the frame with **the locking of your firing hand wrist** down and out like we worked in the grip drill.

CONCLUSION

If you get too "target fixated" you won't notice the sights coming onto the target. Relax your eyes and see as much as you can to notice the sights coming up and toward the target so that they don't surprise you when they get there.

START POSITION

Standing at the 5 m cone, facing down range, holding gun at low ready position, gun fully loaded.

PROCEDURE

Upon start beep or shooter's decision, shooter presents weapon on designated target and fires one round.

Shooter can progress to firing more rounds and add distance.

DO

- Present the pistol to your line of sight.

FEEL

- Your body relaxed at the start and throughout the motion.
- Your arms lock in the pistol and apply recoil management to apply the brakes and stop on target.

SEE

- Notice the sights coming on to target.
- The sights lift and return after every shot.

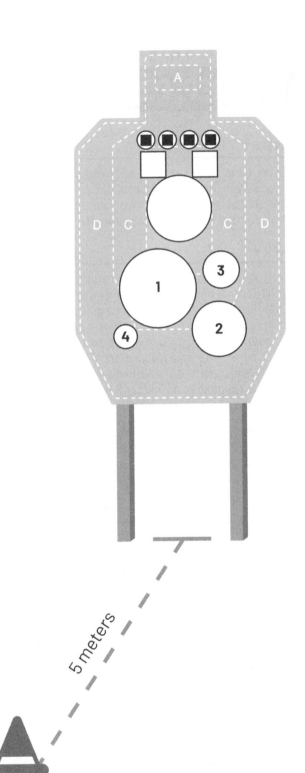

PRESS, PREP, PRESS

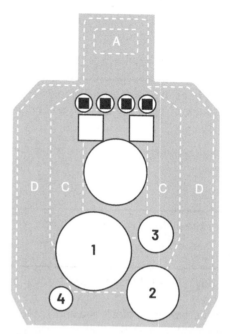

Circles or squares at 5-7 meters

Method	Rounds
Basic	1 in 1.5 seconds
Intermediate	1 in 1.25 seconds
Advanced	1 in 1.0 seconds
Progression: add rounds and distance	2+ at 7+ meters

WHAT

From high ready position, engage a 6" circle with one or two rounds. Ensure you have proper follow-through by resetting the trigger, and maintain recoil management so that the sights re-index back onto target.

WHY

You need to be ready to present your pistol from a multitude of positions. From the holster is definitely important, but you may have the gun out already before needing to take a shot. For a competition shooter, there is only one target on a stage, out of 10 or more, where you engage from the draw. For tactically or home defense minded shooters, you may have to respond to an incident or stimulus with the gun already out.

HOW

Start with the gun broken straight back from full presentation so that the muzzle points upward as it come back. Non Firing hand comes straight back, firing side elbow drops down. Begin with the pistol more or less straight back, and once you have trained this then move the gun higher or lower than your line of sight.

On start, begin **pressing the firing hand** toward target and into your line of site while not moving anything but your arms. Begin to press your non-firing palm by **rotating it into the frame and "torquing"** it forward and down so that the thumb points forward.

As you are pressing the gun forward and up into your line of sight, place the finger on the trigger and take the slack out to the wall so that you are ready to break the shot as soon as the sights are aligned over the target.

Tie the motion of your hands meeting up and torqueing into the frame with **the locking of your firing hand wrist** down and out like we worked in the grip drill.

CONCLUSION

The key here is to make sure your shooting doesn't change at all. You just are taking the little bit extra time to confirm the sights are good enough. Holding on the wall for a split second before breaking the shot could be the difference in a good shot and a bad one.

START POSITION

Standing at the 5 m cone, facing down range, holding gun at high ready position, gun fully loaded.

PROCEDURE

Upon start beep or shooter's decision, shooter presents weapon on designated target and fires one round.

Shooter can progress to firing more rounds and add distance.

DO

- Present the pistol to your line of sight.

FEEL

- Your body relaxed at the start and throughout the motion.
- Your arms lock in the pistol and apply recoil management to apply the brakes and stop on target.

SEE

- Notice the sights coming on to target.
- The sight lift and return after every shot.

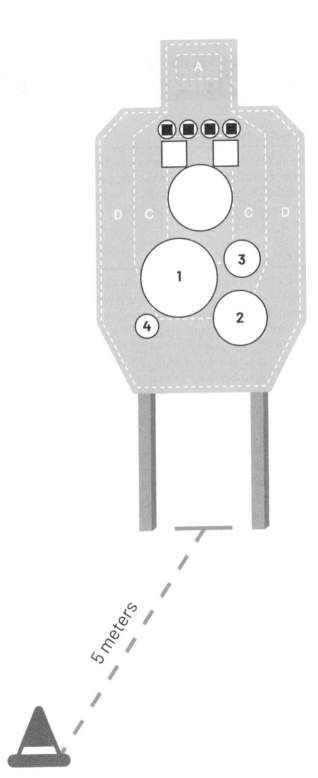

5 meters

UP, ROTATE, PRESS

WHAT

From hand *on* gun and support hand staged around stomach/chest, engage a 6" circle with one round. Ensure you have proper follow through by resetting the trigger, and maintain recoil management so that the sights re-index back onto target.

WHY

When we train the draw without having to get the hand to the gun and defeat retention, we can isolate how we get our sights on target. Here, we find out what we are doing to get the sights lined up consistently.

Common issues we see are that the sights are high and off to the left or right. We need to find what right is, by isolating this portion and feeling our way through it. Most of these issues are fixed simply by how we line up our elbow as our hand is on the gun. Elbow in, sights go outside. Elbow out, sights go inside. Elbow inline, sights are inline. Sights high? Spread the gun as you come out of the holster and concentrate on presenting the pistol so that the slide is flat.

HOW

Start with firing hand in position as you would for your "perfect" grip in the holster, and with your elbow in line with the holster, not flared out. Non-firing hand staged on upper stomach/diaphragm area. Finger is off the trigger and indexed alongside the holster/frame.

On start raise elbow **up** clearing the gun from the holster and **rotate the elbow** forward toward the target so that the slide is parallel to the ground. As the gun rotates forward it should meet the non-firing hand's **touch point** near the hooked index finger.

Press the gun forward toward the target while executing all the focus points of the pressout drill to

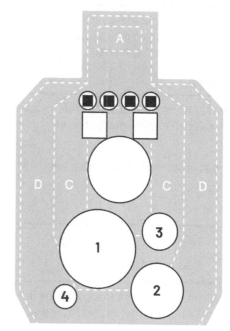

6-8" circle at 7 meters

Method	Rounds
From holster	1 each
Progression: add rounds and distance	2+ at 7+ meters

establish the torque needed to provide proper recoil management before breaking the shot.

Firing hand wrist should lock somewhere between clearing the holster and rotating to a flat slide before meet up.

CONCLUSION

Isolate and diagnose what you need to here. We don't care about speed at first. What's important is that you feel how you are presenting the gun, and know what it takes to get the sights to consistently line up where you are looking.

START POSITION

Standing at the 7 m cone, facing down range, gun is holstered, firing hand on gun, support hand staged on chest/stomach, gun fully loaded.

PROCEDURE

Upon start beep or shooter's decision, shooter presents weapon on designated target and fires one round.

Shooter can progress to firing more rounds and add distance.

DO

- Present the pistol to your line of sight.

FEEL

- The angle of your elbow throughout the draw stroke.
- Your recoil management applied at the very end.

SEE

- How the sights line up at full presentation.
- A flash sight picture as soon as you are able to.

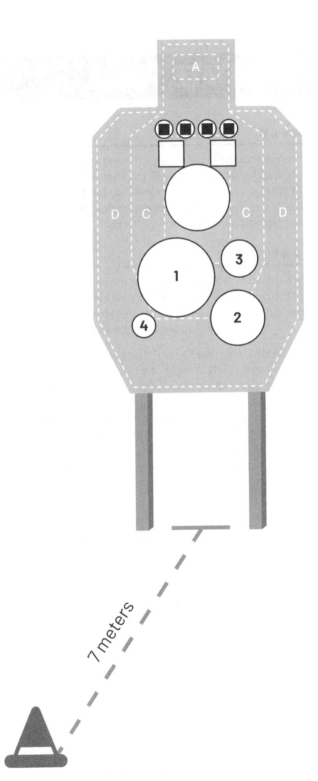

TOUCH, ROTATE, PRESS

WHAT

From hand *off* gun (relaxed at sides or above shoulders), perform three dry runs of getting the hand to gun to establish the three touch points and non firing hand movement to staged position on stomach/diaphragm. After this, engage a 6" circle with one round. Ensure you have proper follow-through by resetting the trigger, and maintain recoil management so that the sights re-index back onto target.

WHY

The firing hand establishing our grip in the holster is what will enable you to be consistent out of the holster and have the best shots possible. This the first critical point of your draw. If it's not right, your performance will be below what you are capable of and have to make corrections through presentation or subsequent shots.

One is better than none, two is better than one, and in this case, three is better than two. Firing hand has three touch points for establishing your grip in the holster and all three need to be achieved. 1) Inside knuckles of the palm, which creates a channel toward a high grip. 2) Knuckle of middle finger, which is your cue to "turnover" and pop out of the holster. 3) Webbing of the hand, which ensures we are high on the backstrap/beavertail and falls into place through the rotation of the gun during the draw. Once these three are achieved we then continue with the draw stroke outlined in the "HOG Draw" drill.

HOW

Start with firing hands relaxed at sides with inside of firing side forearm touching the frame of the gun as an index point, or both hands above shoulders.

To start, perform three dry runs focusing on moving the **elbow back and then in** so that you feel the inside palm funnel hand to alignment, middle knuckle drives into trigger guard, and webbing high on the backstrap.

Once you feel that the grip is established and lined up correctly with your **touch points**, perform a full draw

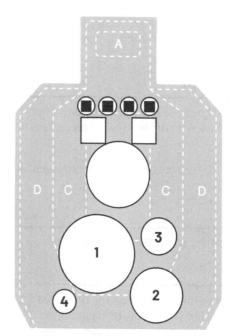

6-8" circle at 7 meters

Method	Rounds
Basic	1 in 1.5 seconds
Intermediate	1 in 1.25 seconds
Advanced	1 in 1.0 seconds
Progression: add rounds and distance	2+ at 7+ meters

just like you did for the "HOG Draw" drill and **press** the gun toward the target.

Tie the motion of your hand turning over, or popping, out of the holster with the touchpoint of the middle knuckle driving into the trigger guard.

CONCLUSION

Now we are putting the draw together. Getting proper placement of the hand on the gun is a critical point of failure, and if not done consistently will cause problems down stream. You may be fast out of the holster, but be careful to not go so fast getting your hand to the gun that you don't have a solid base to accelerate from.

START POSITION

Standing at the 7 m cone, facing down range, gun is holstered, hands relaxed at sides or up, gun fully loaded.

PROCEDURE

Upon start beep or shooter's decision, shooter presents weapon on designated target and fires one round.

Shooter can progress to firing more rounds and add distance.

DO

- Present the pistol to your line of sight.

FEEL

- The three touch points on the firing hand.
- The angle of your elbow throughout the draw stroke.
- Your recoil management applied at the very end.

SEE

- How the sights line up at full presentation.
- A flash sight picture as soon as you are able to.

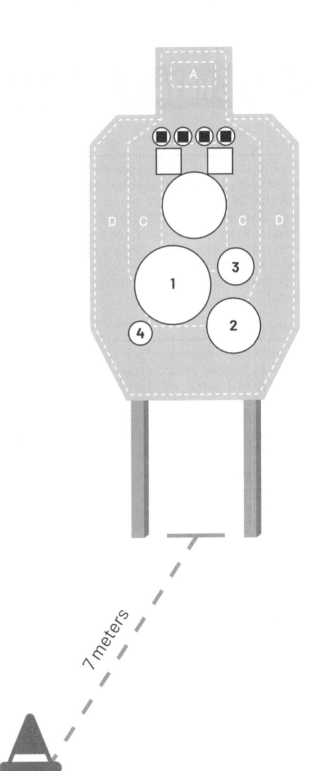

7 meters

DRILL: FULL DRAW
TOUCH, ROTATE, PRESS

1. DROP MAG/TOUCH MAG
2. PAUSE AT INSERT
3. SEND IT HOME

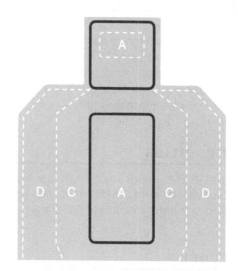

A zone or head box at 7 meters

Method	Rounds
Basic	1R1 in 4 seconds
Intermediate	1R1 in 3 seconds
Advanced	1R1 in 2 seconds
Progression: add rounds and distance	2+ at 7+ meters

WHAT

Starting with gun in holster, round chambered with empty mag in gun, full magazine on standby. Draw and engage A zone or head box with one round, reload and engage with one more round. Bend down and pick up the empty magazine and tac mag it back in the gun to reset the drill.

WHY

Reloading is one of the most practiced pistols skills out there once shooters begin to understand the fundamentals of shooting. Many practice this because it looks cool, but may rarely be exercised in real life during an engagement. If you do need to reload your pistol, you better have it down so it's automated and can get the gun back on target fast. For the competition shooter it is a very needed skill that will save time and help you place higher. For either discipline, if you need to reload then you better be proficient at it because time matters.

For those training on a limited round count, it's a decent way to get mechanics and manipulations in when you don't have a lot of rounds to train with. The two most missed shots are the first off the draw and the first after the reload. Getting your hands set and having everything lined up correctly after manipulating the pistol is something that we have to train to ensure we can take an accurate shot when needed. If you ever find yourself where you need to reload under stress, you are going to wish you were proficient at doing it because you'll probably need to do it fast and proficiently.

HOW

Load up a full magazine and chamber a round. Grasp your empty magazine by placing the baseplate in the palm of your hand, index finger pointed toward the front of the follower, thumb on the side and middle finger on the other side. Now, pinch the mag between index finger and thumb, line up the empty magazine next to the magwell and drop the full mag between your index and middle finger and insert the empty mag to perform a side by side "Tac Mag." Stow the full magazine in your mag pouch and holster the gun.

On start, draw and engage the target with one round, causing the gun to go to slide lock. **Drop mag/ touch mag:** press the mag release with firing hand thumb, while the is gun still mostly up and down and simultaneously grasp the full magazine from your mag carrier with support hand, index finger pointed toward bullets. Touch the mag release and new mag at the same time.

Bring the magazine up to where it naturally lines up as the hand rotates toward the magwell, simultaneously rotating the magwell toward the mag so you can see the inside of it while staging the firing thumb on the slide release. **Pause at insert.** Insert the new magazine and push the frame up while seating the mag to release the slide. **Send it home.** Continue to let the non firing hand travel upwards to establish your grip and press the gun back on target, acquiring the sights and taking the second shot as the sights line up. If you can't reach the slide release with your firing hand thumb, use your support hand thumb.

CONCLUSION

Know where to go fast, and where to slow down. Pausing at insert is where we don't want to rush. Take a split second to make sure this is done correctly. We want reloads to be automated to the point when you go to slide lock, you immediately go into your reload. Every time you load and make ready is a good time to get a little reload dry practice in.

START POSITION

Standing at the 7 m cone, facing down range, gun is holstered, hands relaxed at sides or up, gun has round chambered with empty magazine, full magazine in carrier.

PROCEDURE

Upon start beep or shooter's decision, draw and fire 1 round, reload from slide lock, and fire another round into target. Pick up empty magazine and tac mag in to reset for the drill.

Shooter can progress to firing more rounds and add distance.

DO

- Swipe the new mag quickly
- Pause at insert to ensure the mag is lined up.
- Reestablish proper grip after reload.

FEEL

- The difference in recoil impulse when the slide locks to rear.
- Your support hand grab the new magazine as you depress the mag release.
- Your hands reestablish proper grip after reload.

SEE

- The inside of the magwellas you pause at insert.
- The sights line up correctly after reload.

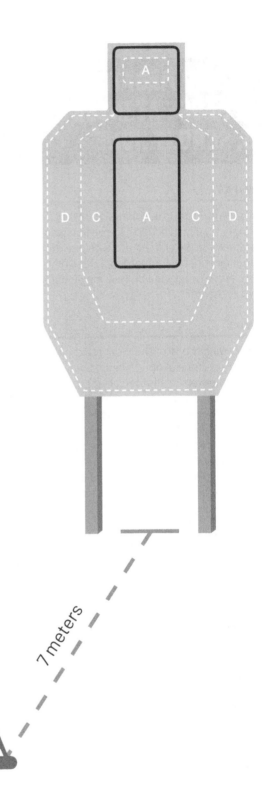

DRILL: TAC MAG/COMBAT RELOADS
1. DROP MAG/TOUCH MAG, 2. PAUSE AT INSERT, 3. SEND IT HOME

SLAP, RACK, RELOAD

WHAT

Starting with gun in holster, round chambered with empty mag in gun, empty mag on standby, and full mag as secondary, draw and engage a 6" circle with one round, reload empty mag and perform slap/rack malfunction clearance, reload with full mag, and engage with one more round. Bend down and pick up the empty magazines, tac mag it back in the gun, stow full and other empty mag to reset the drill.

WHY

It's important to be able to differentiate, and practice, between a reload and a malfunction. When we feel that we need to reload we want to know the gun is out of bullets, and when we get a click we want to be sure that there is a malfunction issue. We should know the gun is out of ammo because it doesn't go to slide lock. If this doesn't happen, and we begin to reload, we may waste time performing this when in actuality we should have been working toward clearing the stoppage. If the gun goes down in a fight, we need to get it back up as quickly as possible.

This drill is a low round count drill to work on your mechanics and make the "SLAP, RACK" malfunction clearance second nature. If you get a "CLICK" you slap the mag and rack the slide. If you get a difference in recoil impulse and notice that the slide is fully locked to the rear then you need to reload. We should grasp and manipulate the gun in a way that ensures there is no guess work.

HOW

Everything is the same as the previous drill, the only thing we are adding is the empty mag between the first shot and the full mag. When you reload the empty mag, you can use a dummy round or spent piece of brass to make the slide go forward more easily if you want. If not, just keep the magazine empty. Little harder to send the slide forward but it will still work.

On start, draw and engage the target with one round, causing the gun to go to slide lock. Reload in your empty magazine and send the slide forward. Fire the gun and recognize the "CLICK" of a misfire/

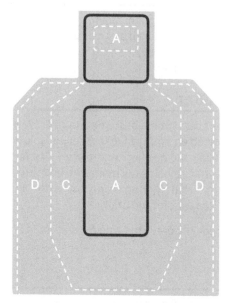

A zone or head box at 7 meters

Method	Rounds
Basic	1R0R1 in 6 seconds
Intermediate	1R0R1 in 5 seconds
Advanced	1R0R1 in 4 seconds
Progression: add rounds and distance	2+ at 7+ meters

malfunction. Rotate the mag well into the non-firing hand while slapping the bottom of the magazine to ensure it's seated. Rotate the slide back over in the non-firing hand and rack the slide from the front or the rear. When slide locks back, perform another reload with your full magazine and shoot the second round. Kneel down with gun at the high ready and perform tac mag to reset the drill.

CONCLUSION

We're only working the process of slapping the bottom of the mag and racking the slide here. We need to get into the habit of this being habitual when the gun doesn't fire. Will slap/rack solve a malfunction? Maybe. If not, then "Slap, Lock, Drop" then clear what you got and get it back into operation.

START POSITION

Standing at the 7 m cone, facing down range, gun is holstered, hands relaxed at sides or up, gun has round chambered with empty magazine, empty mag and full magazine in carrier.

PROCEDURE

Upon start beep or shooter's decision, draw and fire 1 round, reload an empty mag from slide lock, when you feel the click and no shot immediately slap and rack to check it, then reload a full magazine and fire another round into target. Pick up empty magazine and tac mag it in to reset for the drill.

Shooter can progress to firing more rounds and add distance.

DO

- Swipe the new mag quickly
- SLAP and RACK when you get click not bang.

FEEL

- The difference in recoil impulse when the slide locks to rear.
- The difference in no round being fired.
- The bottom of the mag slaping against your support palm before racking the slide.

SEE

- The inside of the magwell as you pause at insert.
- The sights line up correctly after reload.

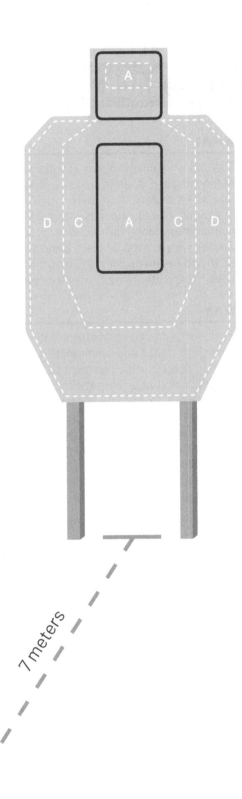

7 meters

DRILL: RELOAD MALFUNCTION
SLAP, RACK, RELOAD

TIE YOUR DRAW STROKE TO YOUR STEPS, THEN FULL DRAW IN FEWER STEPS

WHAT

From hand *off* gun (relaxed at sides or above shoulders), while taking three steps and simultaneously draw your gun and fire at target on or after the third step. You will move forward, right and left of your target.

WHY

Anything we do static we want to translate to movement. This is part of our variable training and we need to ensure that we can draw the gun through movement as well. As you start to move, we usually see a drop in our draw time by 0.25-0.5 seconds because our focus in on the movement. Because angles change with the direction we are moving and as the hips shift in our gait, you need to train this so it is as comfortable and natural as drawing when static.

HOW

Start with firing hands relaxed at sides, up at the interview position or transition position in your good shooting stance.

You will start and finish squared up to the target whether you are moving forward, 30 degrees left, or 30 degrees to the right. Begin your draw simultaneously as you take your first step, tying each of the 3 draw positions into each of the three steps.

- Step 1: Hand on gun
- Step 2: Rotate to flat
- Step 3: Press sights onto target

Take your shot once you are settled into position after the third step. Once you can comfortably draw your gun, tying your draw to each step, progress by getting to full draw in 2 steps or even quicker than that. Track your target and time the shot as you land your third step instead of settling into target.

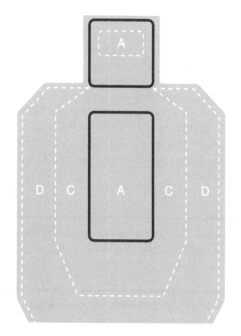

A zone or head box at 7 meters

Method	Rounds
Forward	1–3 varied
Left	1–3 varied
Right	1–3 varied
Progression: add rounds and distance	1–3 varied

CONCLUSION

Get comfortable with drawing the gun during movement, presenting the gun on target while moving, and eventually tracking the target until you stop to shoot. Here we take what we did static, and translate it to moving.

START POSITION

Standing at the 7 m cone, facing down range, gun is loaded and holstered, hands relaxed at sides or up.

PROCEDURE

Upon buzzer, simultaneously draw and move toward the indicated direction and have gun and sights presented on target within 3 steps. Take your shots once you have settled into position and squared up to the targets. Scan, perform tac-mag reload, and move back to the start.

DO

- Find a consistent touch point on your draw.
- Orient your torso toward the target while moving.

FEEL

- The inside of your palm funnel your hand to the gun.
- The ground as you move to avoid excess motion.
- Yourself framing the gun out while moving.

SEE

- The sights track the target through movement.
- The sight lift and reset the same way.

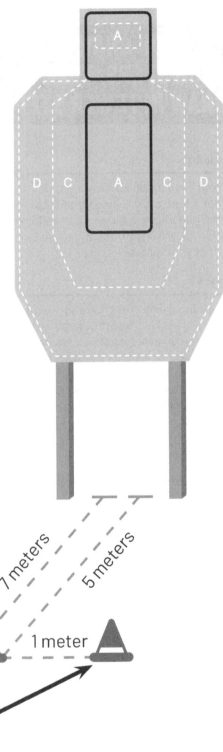

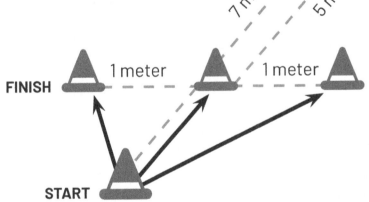

DRILL: 3 STEP DRAW

TIE YOUR DRAW STROKE TO YOUR STEPS, THEN FULL DRAW IN FEWER STEPS

SIGHTS AND TRIGGER RESET FAST, USE THE REST OF THE TIME TO REFINE SIGHTS

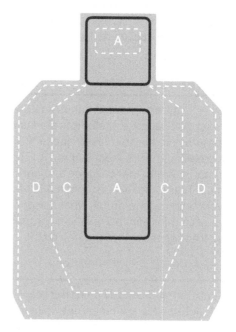

A zone or head box at 7 meters

Method	Rounds
3 meters	5 at <0.25 splits
7 meters	5 at <0.50 splits
15 meters	5 at <0.75 splits
25 meters	5 at <1.00 splits

WHAT

From the draw, engage the upper half of an IPSC A zone with 5 rounds from the distance and cadence listed above. Goal is to get all five rounds in the target in the splits listed *at a minimum*.

WHY

The purpose of moving back to distance is to recognize the size of the target in relation to your sights, irons, or red dot. The goal is for the shooter to be ready as fast as possible after each shot, trigger reset and sights back on target, so that you have as much of the time available to you to refine your sight picture as needed. At closer distances there is less focal shift needed to refine the sight picture, farther back where the target is smaller in relation to the sights you will have more time between shots to refine the sight picture for more accuracy. The faster you reset the trigger and get sights back on target, the more time you will have to confirm your sights. The faster you confirm your sights, the less time you will need to take the shot which will result in speed.

HOW

Start with gun in holster, draw and fire 5 rounds onto the target with the goal of getting all 5 rounds in the upper A Zone of the target. Use the cadences below for starting points for each distance.

Hammer Cadence: 3 meters | 12345 | "As fast as you can pull the trigger"
½ Cadence: 7 meters | 1,2,3,4,5, | *"bang, bang, bang..."*
¾ Cadence: 15 meters | 1, and 2, and 3, | *"bang and bang and bang..."*
Full Cadence: 25 meters | 1 thousand, 2 thousand, ... | *"bang,* thousand *bang,* thousand..."

If you can achieve all the rounds in the target zone consistently, then use a faster cadence at that distance. If one round is out then keep the same cadence. If more than one round is out then use a slower cadence.

At the fastest cadence you will most likely not feel yourself resetting the trigger and taking the slack out. As more time is allotted between shots you will feel the wall of the trigger and break the shot on initial sound of the number. All fundamentals established in the now drill and recoil management drill are applied here.

CONCLUSION

The longer and faster you can see your sights through recoil the better you'll get. Then get to the point of seeing your sights draw a straight line up and down to the same point with each shot. The straighter that line is, the more accurate you'll be.

START POSITION

Standing at prescribed distance, facing down range, gun is loaded and holstered, hands relaxed at sides or up.

PROCEDURE

Upon buzzer, draw and shoot 5 rounds into the A Zone at the prescribed cadence. If all shots are inside the A Zone, progress to the next faster cadence and/or focus on breaking the first shot sooner. If 1 shot is outside, continue with that cadence and work to get all in. If more than 1 shot is outside the A Zone, switch to a slower cadence to reinforce what correct is and so that you can think and feel your way through the drill, as well as see the sights through recoil.

DO

- Find a consistent touch point on your draw.
- Orient your torso toward the target while moving.

FEEL

- The inside of your palm funnel your hand to the gun.
- The ground as you move to avoid excess motion.
- Yourself framing the gun out while moving.

SEE

- The sights track the target through movement.
- The sight lift and reset the same way.

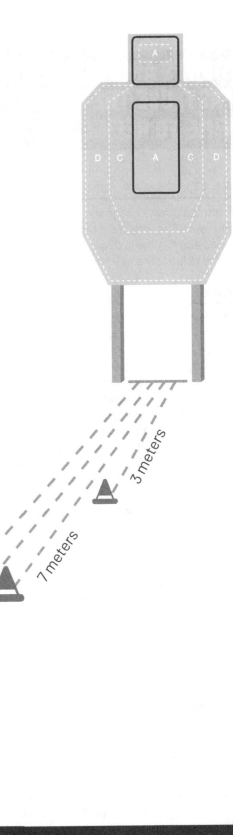

EYES LEAD GUN, RESET TRIGGER ON NEXT TARGET

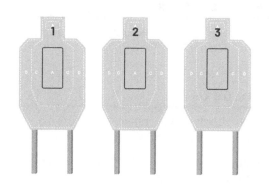

A zone at 7 meters

Method	Rounds
1-0-1	2 at 0.5 splits
1-1-1	3 at 0.35 splits
2-0-2	4 at 0.5 splits
2-2-2	6 at 0.35 splits

WHAT

Targets are set up at 7 meters with 1 meter between each target. Similar to USPSA "El Prez" Classifier drill. Draw and engage targets with the round counts listed.

WHY

This drill is not "how do I shoot three bad guys in front of me," but instead is to focus on the transitions between each target. There are two types of transitions, near and far. Near target transitions you only need to RESET YOUR TRIGGER on the next target with minimal effort from the body and hips. Far target transitions you need to DRIVE YOUR HIPS to get the gun onto the next target.

If you train how fast you can shoot on target, you will ignore the transitions and time it takes to get from target to target. To focus on the transition and do it quickly, you may need to slow down the splits on target. Once you can isolate the transition, then your splits on target and between target should be within 0.05 of each other. The consistency doing this will translate into better overall times. We do this so that as soon as we have solved the problem in front of us, we can see and then drive the gun as fast as possible to the next target where we are looking. We gain more speed between targets than on them. Know when you can go fast, and know when you need to take your time. To do this, the eyes need to break out of the sights and lead the gun onto the next target.

HOW

Start with gun in holster, draw and fire with the goal of getting all the rounds in the A Zone of the target. Use the cadences below for starting points for each distance.

Far Target Transition: 1-0-1 | T1 x 1 rd, T3 x 1 rd
Near Target Transitions: 1-1-1 | T1 x 1 rd, T2 x 1 rd, T3 x 1 rd
Far TgtTransition: 2-0-2 | T1 x 2 rds, T3 x 2 rds
Near TgtTransitions: 2-2-2 | T1 x 2 rds, T2 x 2 rds, T3 x 2 rds

The main focus here is the eyes and how we see. When you take your last shot on target, the eyes immediately drive to the next and the gun follows by resetting the trigger on the next target.

For far target transitions, you need to use the hips to drive the gun because now your torso will be out of alignment with your hips at this distance. Don't push the gun or lean toward the next target. Instead, twist your hips to move your entire torso onto it so that you are squared up onto the next target.

CONCLUSION

As soon as you call your last shot good, snap eyes immediately to next target feel the wall of your trigger as the sights enter the next target.recoil the better you'll get. Then get to the point of seeing your sights draw a straight line up and down to the same point with each shot. The straighter that line is, the more accurate you'll be.

START POSITION

Standing at prescribed distance, facing down range, gun is loaded and holstered, hands relaxed at sides or up.

PROCEDURE

Upon buzzer, draw and engage all targets as prescribed below for "NEAR" and "FAR" transitions.

Far Target Transition: 1-0-1 | T1 x 1 rd, T3 x 1 rd
Near Target Transitions: 1-1-1 | T1 x 1 rd, T2 x 1 rd, T3 x 1 rd
Far TgtTransition: 2-0-2 | T1 x 2 rds, T3 x 2 rds
Near TgtTransitions: 2-2-2 | T1 x 2 rds, T2 x 2 rds, T3 x 2 rds

DO

• Isolate the transition. Place focus there rather than the splits on target.

FEEL

• The gun snap onto the next target.
• Your hips drive the gun on far target transitions.
• Yourself reset the trigger on the next target.

SEE

• The next target and the sights being tethered behind the eyes.
• See the sight lift and reset the same way.

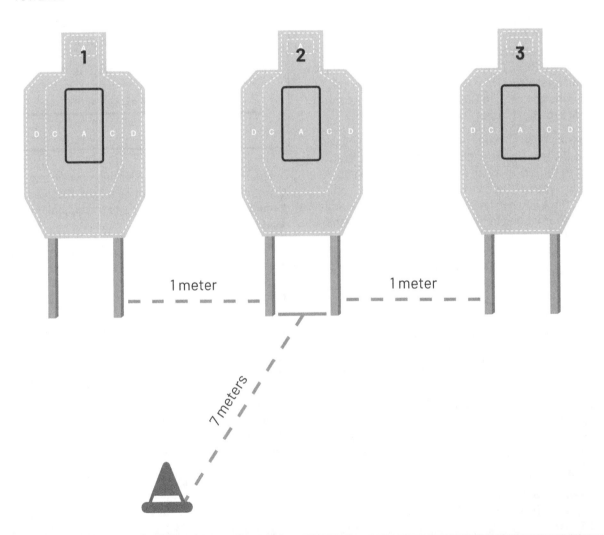

DRILL: MULTI TARGET TRANSITIONS
EYES LEAD GUN, RESET TRIGGER ON NEXT TARGET

SIZE OF TARGET COMPARED TO SIGHT, TELLS YOU HOW MUCH ACCURACY YOU NEED

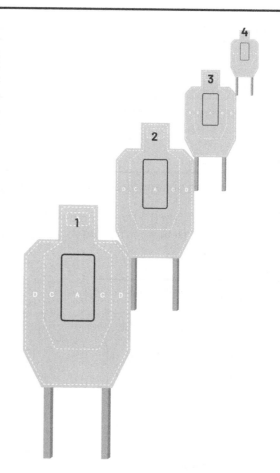

WHAT

Either IPSC, AC Zone steel, or a combination of targets are set up in succession away from shooter at 5, 10, 15, and 25 meters. Upon buzzer, shooter engages first target, then second, first, third, first, fourth, and first with 2 rounds each. Alternate set up is with the second page of the BAER Warm Up Target and engages the circles in the order of 1, 2, 1, 3, 1, 4, 1 from a set distance. Other option, perform in reverse order.

WHY

Knowing when to speed up and when to slow down is a common saying we hear a lot. Recognizing the target in relation to your sights and taking only as much time as needed to be accurate is how we can train that.

HOW

Start with gun in holster, draw and fire with the goal of getting all the rounds in the A Zone of each target.

The main focus here recognizing the size of the target in relation to our sights. If the target is smaller then you will need more time to ensure an accurate shot, target is larger in relation to the sight and you need less time.

CONCLUSION

As soon as you call your last shot good, snap eyes immediately to next target feel the wall of your trigger as the sights enter the next target.

A zone at 5, 10, 15, 25 meters

Method	Rounds
1, 2, 1, 3, 1, 4, 1	1 or 2 per target
4, 3, 4, 2, 4, 1, 4	1 or 2 per target
Progression: Add LPs	

START POSITION

Standing at the cone, facing down range. Gun holstered and loaded.

PROCEDURE

Upon buzzer, draw and engage all targets as prescribed above for "near" and "far" transitions.

DO

- Isolate the transition and place focus there rather than the splits on target.
- Recognize the size of the target compared to sight, and how much sight picture you need to engage accurately.

FEEL

- The gun snap onto the next target.
- Your hips drive the gun on far target transitions
- Yourself reset the trigger on the next target.

SEE

- The size of the target in relation to your sights.
- The next target and the sights being tethered behind the eyes.
- The sight lift and reset the same way.

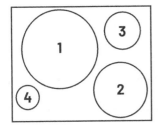

Alternate TGT: BAER W/U page 2

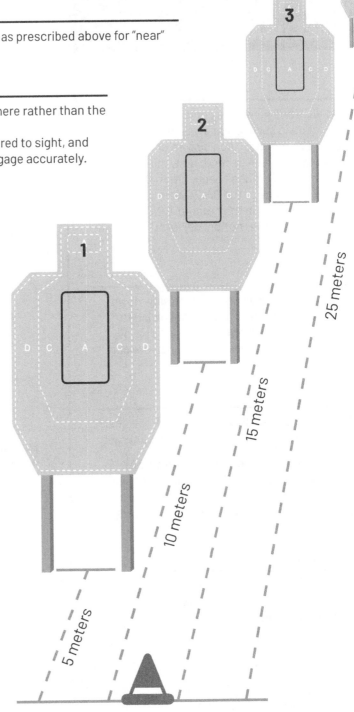

SIZE OF TARGET COMPARED TO SIGHT, TELLS YOU HOW MUCH ACCURACY YOU NEED

DRILL: EL PREZ 2.0

EYES LEAD GUN, RESET TRIGGER ON NEXT TARGET

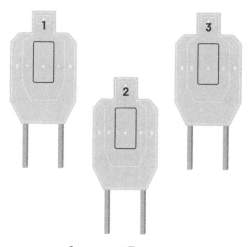

A zone at 7 meters

Method	Rounds
T1, T2, T1, T3, T1	3 each
Progression: Vary round count and order	3 each

WHAT

Targets are set up at 7 meters with 1 meter between each target. Similar to USPSA "El Prez" Classifier drill. Draw and engage targets with the round counts listed.

WHY

This drill is similar to the "Target Transition" drill earlier, now we are adding more rounds, farther separation and a different order to add another level of complexity.

As we add more rounds, we require more focus and stamina to ensure we maintain recoil management throughout the whole drill.

HOW

Start with gun in holster, draw and fire with the goal of getting all the rounds in the A Zone of the target. Use the order above to engage each one.

The main focus here is the eyes and how we see. When you take your last shot on target, the eyes immediately drive to the next and the gun follows by resetting the trigger on the next target.

For the target transitions, you need to use the hips to drive the gun because now your torso will be out of alignment with your hips at this distance. Don't push the gun or lean toward the next target. Instead, twist your hips to move your entire torso onto it so that you are squared up onto the next target.

CONCLUSION

As soon as you call your last shot good, snap eyes immediately to next target feel the wall of your trigger as the sights enter the next target.

START POSITION

Standing in Box A facing down or up range.

PROCEDURE

Upon buzzer, draw and engage T1 x 3 rds, T2 x 3 rds, T1 x 3 rds, T3 x 3 rds, T1 x 3 rds in each target's A Zone.

Progression: If you have a training partner or someone who can change the targets while you aren't looking, you can add in non-threat and threat targets to work target identification.

DO

- Isolate the transition. Place focus there rather than the splits on target.

FEEL

- The gun snap onto the next target.
- Your hips drive the gun on far target transitions.
- Yourself reset the trigger on the next target.

SEE

- The next target and the sights being tethered behind the eyes.
- See the sight lift and reset the same way.

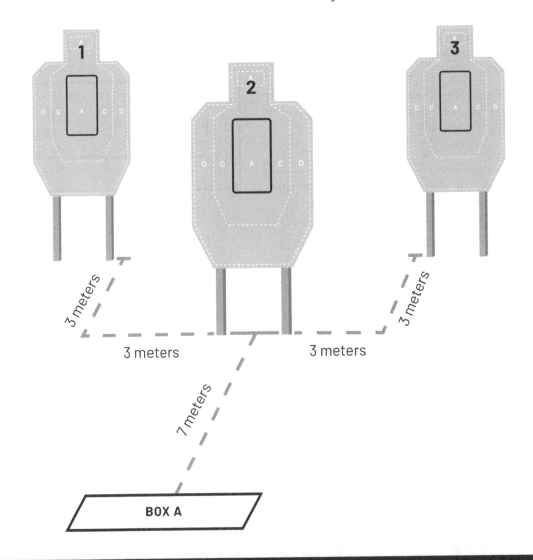

3 meters

3 meters

3 meters

3 meters

7 meters

BOX A

EYES LEAD GUN, RESET TRIGGER ON NEXT TARGET

SIZE OF TARGET COMPARED TO SIGHT, TELLS YOU HOW MUCH ACCURACY YOU NEED

WHAT

9 USPSA or similar silhouette style targets are set up in a diamond shape so that each a zone (or partial A Zone) is visible from at least one position in the shooting area. Right edge of the shooting area is inline with right most target, same for the left side. Barrier in the middle is the starting point with hands on wall. Rules: only TGT 1 can be shot in the head, TGT's 4 and 6 must be shot from the opposite sides. 4 from the right side, 6 from the left side.

WHY

In every safety brief it states "know what's in front of and behind your target." Rarely do we ever practice this and force ourselves to be accountable in this regard. We have to think in 3D, not just the 2D that we usually experience on the flat range. Work on visualizing the environment in depth and using what information you can to draw the lines of where the target behind it overlaps.

HOW

Start with gun loaded and holstered, hands on wall. Shooting commands are Order, Direction, Beep. Engage the targets as prescribed with 2 rounds each.

The main focus here is seeing in depth, building that mental picture to effectively thread the needle for the shots, and being confident in your ability to take the shot when it may not be ideal. There may be an easier shot elsewhere, but your ability and confidence should tell you whether to take it or find a better option.

CONCLUSION

You have to be accountable for every round that goes into the gun, and every round that comes out of it. Seeing in depth and being accountable for where the round will go after you shoot, is a level you need to achieve.

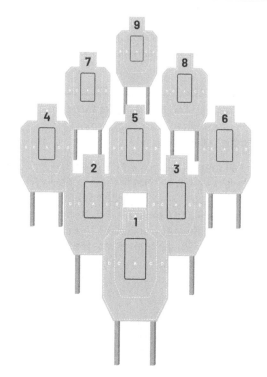

A zone at 10-15 meters

Method	Rounds
1-9, Left or Right	2 per target
9-1, Left or Right	2 per target
Progression: Add colors, odds, evens	2 per target

START POSITION

Standing within the shooting area behind cover, facing down range, hands on X's.

PROCEDURE

Timer calls out "Standby", order of targets "1-9/9-1", direction to start engagement "Left/Right", then "Beep".

Engage all targets in order with 2 rounds ea. All targets must be shot in the A Zone, except for Target 1 which may be shot in the head. Targets 4 and 6 must be shot from the opposite side of the barricade from the side it is on. 4 from the right, 6 from the left. Reload behind cover and do not go outside the shooting box.

DO

- Thread the needle so your round impacts somewhere in the A Zone, avoiding other targets.
- Reload behind cover.
- Engage the correct targets in order, all others are considered non-threats.

FEEL

- Where you are within the shooting area.

SEE

- What is in front of and behind your target.

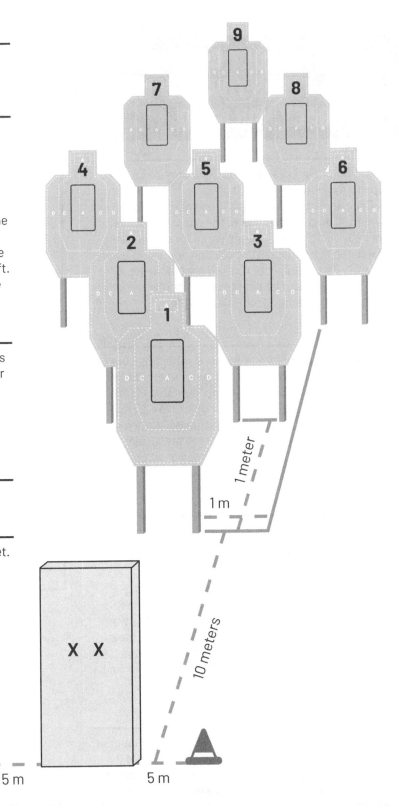

DRILL: BAER THROUGH IT

SIZE OF TARGET COMPARED TO SIGHT, TELLS YOU HOW MUCH ACCURACY YOU NEED

SNAPSHOT, HANDS, AIM, SHOOT

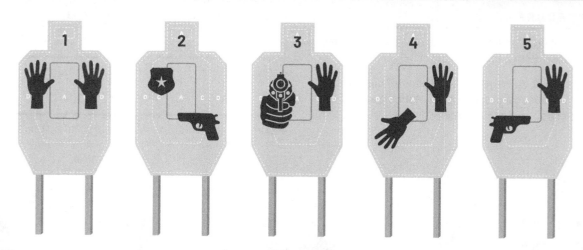

A zone at 7 and 3 meters

Method	Rounds
Engage all from 7 meters	2 per target
Engage all from 3 meters	2 per target
Progression: Add distance and other cue	2 per target

WHAT

5 targets with, separated by 1 meter between each target, with varying threat and non-threat cues on each. Two distances to shoot from at 7 and 3 meters from the middle target.

WHY

It's important to know what's in front of and behind your target, it's equally if not more important to ensure we only engage the correct target. We have to see and confirm our target before we engage it.

HOW

Start with gun loaded and holstered, hands on wall. On beep or command to begin, turn and shoot all threat targets only. Engage the center mass of the targets as prescribed with a minimum of 2 rounds each.

After each run, have training partner mix up the targets and/or add new ones. Use threat and non threat targets, or can use cutouts of guns, knives, badges, phones, hands or other visual cues.

CONCLUSION

Work your process, and solve one problem at a time.

START POSITION

String 1, standing in Box A facing up range. String 2, standing in Box B facing up range.

PROCEDURE

Upon buzzer, turn and engage all threat targets only in any order with 2 rounds each.

Timer will set up targets with either stencils, printed paper, or reusable props of guns, hands, badges, or knives in any way or order they desire.

DO

- Work your process of hands, aim, shoot.
- Keep your eyes out of sights during transition from target to target.
- Aim center mass and not at visual cues.

FEEL

- What you need for good target transitions.

SEE

- The next target before your sights line up on it.

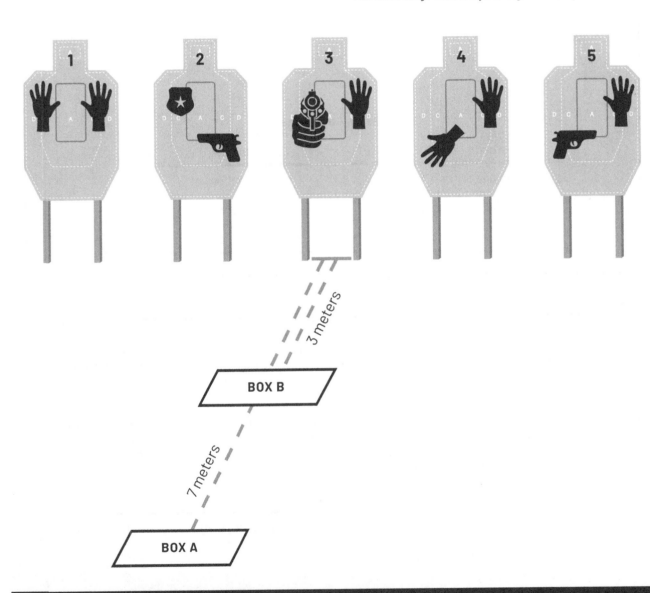

MEASURE YOUR ABILITY FROM A COLD START

WHAT

Target is placed 3, 5, or 7 meters from shooter.

WHY

We need to be able to measure our ability from a cold start. In real life you don't have the ability to warm up. It's imperative we know where our line between success and failure is, and train that to perform at higher levels from a cold status.

In this drill we want to see what your dray time is through a multiple round string, how recoil management holds up through 10 rounds with a transition in the middle, reload, then the ability to slow down and make accurate shots.

This drill serves as a diagnostic in classes to see where shooters stand skill wise, and what we need to put focus on.

HOW

10 round mag loaded in the gun, 2 full magazines on standby, facing down range at prescribed distance, hands relaxed at sides or up.

On buzzer, draw and engage each grey rectangle with 5 rounds each, perform a slide lock or empty chamber reload, then fire 3 rounds at the center circle. Once you have fired all your rounds, perform scan and tac mag a fresh mag into the pistol.

Focus on making the first shot count and then maintain focus on recoil management throughout the whole drill. It's easy to speed up, but hard to slow down. Once you reload, ensure you get the proper touch points and consistent grip to put three accurate rounds on target.

Once the firing is complete, perform your scan and tac mag a new magazine into the gun.

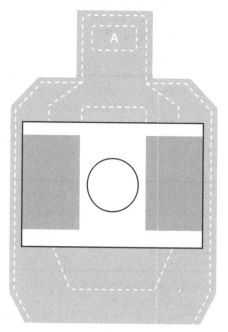

BAER Standard at 3/5/7 meters

Method	Rounds
3 meters	13 in 9 seconds
5 meters	13 in 9 seconds
7 meters	13 in 9 seconds
Progression: do it faster	13 in ? seconds

CONCLUSION

For a fairly simple 13 round drill, there is a lot going on here. A lot of people think about what they need to do coming up, and not what they are doing at that moment. Break it up into smaller sections and perform one task at a time.

START POSITION

Standing in Box A facing down range. 10 round mag loaded, 2 full mags on standby.

PROCEDURE

Upon buzzer, draw and engage each grey rectangle with 5 rounds each, performs a slide lock or empty chamber reload, and fire 3 rounds into the center circle. Once shooting is complete, scan and tac mag.

DO

- Focus on one task at a time.
- Throttle control for critical points like reload and accurate rounds.

FEEL

- The support hand gripping and driving the gun throughout the shot string.
- The wall of the trigger as you break your accurate rounds.

SEE

- The sight lift after each shot to call it good.
- The size of the target in relation to sights to determine how accurate you need to be related to your speed.

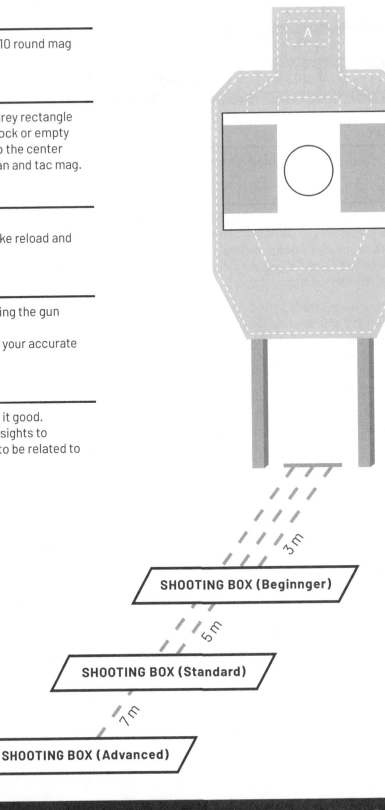

SHOOTING BOX (Beginnger)

3 m

SHOOTING BOX (Standard)

5 m

SHOOTING BOX (Advanced)

7 m

DRILL: BAER STANDARD

MEASURE YOUR ABILITY FROM A COLD START

FUNDAMENTALS EXECUTED FLAWLESSLY EVERY TIME

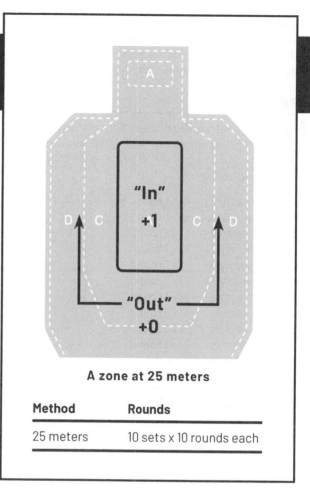

A zone at 25 meters

Method	Rounds
25 meters	10 sets x 10 rounds each

WHAT

Target is placed 25 meters from shooter. You will draw and shoot 100 rounds as prescribed below, and score it after every 10 rounds.

WHY

This drill originally was told to me from another instructor named Matt, who heard it from Dave Dawson, who was told by another person. In Dave's words, "if you score 95 or higher on this drill, you probably have the skills to be a USPSA GM." Can't really argue with that, and after doing this for several months it becomes addictive in a way.

I've found that this drill teaches you a lot about trusting the shot, calling the shot, and making sure you prep and pull the trigger correctly each time.

HOW

From 25 meters, facing down range, you will draw and shoot after each round, or 2 rounds as depicted below. After each shot, feel the wall of the trigger and reset the sights and trigger as if you were going to take another shot before holstering.

After each 10 round set, go to the target and score how many hits you got out of 10. Inside the A zone is a point, outside is 0 points. Mark off your hits and misses with a sharpie or pasters, I like to score it by writing it on the head box of the target.

1. Freestyle   10 x 1 round
2. Freestyle   10 x 1 round
3. Freestyle   10 x 1 round
4. Freestyle   10 x 1 round
5. Freestyle   10 x 1 round
6. Freestyle   10 x 1 round
7. Freestyle   10 x 1 round
8. Freestyle   10 x 1 round
9. Freestyle   10 x 1 round
10. Freestyle   10 x 1 round

CONCLUSION

Maintain focus and if you pull a shot, move on and don't worry about it. Know why you pulled it, and remember that next time. Progress not perfection.

START POSITION

Standing at 25 meter cone facing down range, gun loaded to full capacity and holstered.

PROCEDURE

Upon buzzer, draw and engage A zone as prescribed below and reset sights and trigger back to wall after each shot. Holster and engage from draw after each prescribed string.

1. Freestyle   10 x 1 round
2. Freestyle   10 x 1 round
3. Freestyle   10 x 1 round
4. Freestyle   10 x 1 round
5. Freestyle   10 x 1 round
6. Freestyle   10 x 1 round
7. Freestyle   10 x 1 round
8. Freestyle   10 x 1 round
9. Freestyle   10 x 1 round
10. Freestyle   10 x 1 round

DO

- Maintain focus for every string and shot.
- Treat each shot as individual.
- Remember this is not about time, it's about doing it right every time.

FEEL

- Your solid base and frames so that you can touch the target.
- The trigger break at the moment the sight is where you want it.

SEE

- The sight lift and return, drawing a straight line up and back down.

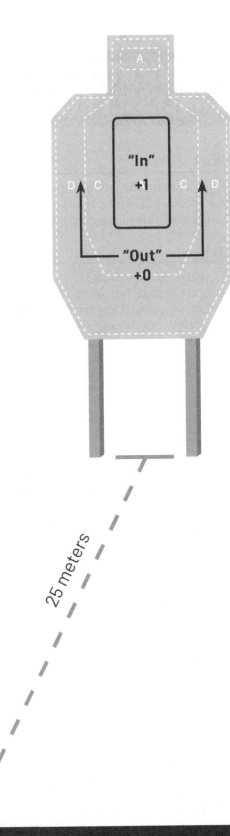

FUNDAMENTALS EXECUTED FLAWLESSLY EVERY TIME

WHAT

Target is placed 25 meters from shooter. You will draw and shoot 100 rounds as prescribed below, and score it after every 10 rounds.

WHY

This drill originally was told to me from another instructor named Matt, who heard it from Dave Dawson, who was told by another person. In Dave's words, "if you score 95 or higher on this drill, you probably have the skills to be a USPSA GM." Can't really argue with that, and after doing this for several months it becomes addictive in a way.

I've found that this drill teaches you a lot about trusting the shot, calling the shot, and making sure you prep and pull the trigger correctly each time.

After running the original version of this, we started running a modified version of it that you see here. Now we are adding 2 rounds to the sets, as well as firing one handed with 1 and 2 rounds. It serves not only as a confidence builder, but really hones in on the small things you need to focus on to be successful.

HOW

From 25 meters, facing down range, you will draw and shoot after each round, or 2 rounds as depicted below. After each shot, feel the wall of the trigger and reset the sights and trigger as if you were going to take another shot before holstering.

After each 10 round set, go to the target and score how many hits you got out of 10. Inside the A zone is a point, outside is 0 points. Mark off your hits and misses with a sharpie or pasters, I like to score it by writing it on the head box of the target.

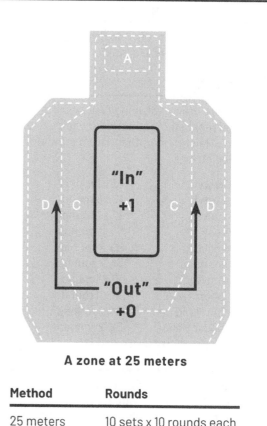

A zone at 25 meters

Method	Rounds
25 meters	10 sets x 10 rounds each

1. Freestyle — 10 x 1 round
2. Freestyle — 10 x 1 round
3. Freestyle — 10 x 1 round
4. Freestyle — 5 x 2 rounds
5. Freestyle — 5 x 2 rounds
6. Freestyle — 5 x 2 rounds
7. Firing Hand — 10 x 1 round
8. Support Hand — 10 x 1 round
9. Firing Hand — 5 x 2 rounds
10. Support Hand — 5 x 2 rounds

CONCLUSION

Maintain focus and if you pull a shot, move on and don't worry about it. Know why you pulled it, and remember that next time. Progress not perfection.

START POSITION

Standing at 25 meter cone facing down range, gun loaded to full capacity and holstered.

PROCEDURE

Upon buzzer, draw and engage A zone as prescribed below and reset sights and trigger back to wall after each shot. Holster and engage from draw after each prescribed string.

1.	Freestyle	10 x 1 round
2.	Freestyle	10 x 1 round
3.	Freestyle	10 x 1 round
4.	Freestyle	5 x 2 rounds
5.	Freestyle	5 x 2 rounds
6.	Freestyle	5 x 2 rounds
7.	Firing Hand	10 x 1 round
8.	Support Hand	10 x 1 round
9.	Firing Hand	5 x 2 rounds
10.	Support Hand	5 x 2 rounds

DO

- Maintain focus for every string and shot.
- Treat each shot as individual.
- Remember this is not about time, it's about doing it right every time.

FEEL

- Your solid base and frames so that you can touch the target.
- The trigger break at the moment the sight is where you want it.

SEE

- The sight lift and return, drawing a straight line up and back down.

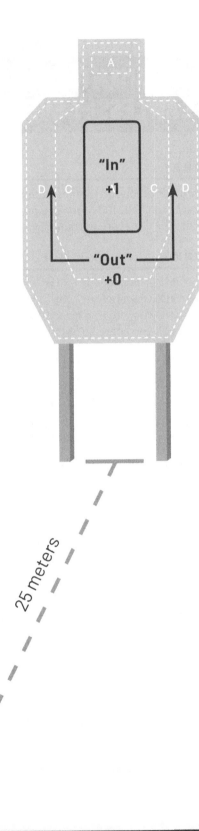

SPREAD, TORQUE, WEDGE

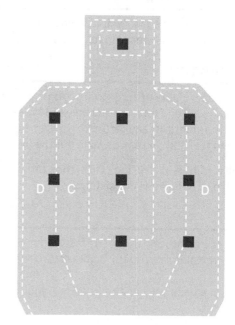

1" pasters at 3m

Method	Rounds
Both Hands, or single hand	2-3 strings
Repeat for 10 strings, 1 string/paster	Total: 20-30

WHAT

Starting with the pistol on paster, fire 2 or 3 rds at a comfortable pace applying the most recoil management needed to have the sights return to the same index point. Start easy and then pick up speed to fine tune the recoil management applied. Goal is to have all rounds touching the paster for each string of fire.

WHY

Recoil management is one half of being "shooter ready" as JJ Racaza calls it. The trigger portion was addressed in the Now Drill. If each time you pull the trigger you know where the gun will return, or re-index to, then you can take the guess work out of your shots and trust your shooting more.

Your goal here is for the sights to re-index back onto the same spot so that all rounds are in the paster.

HOW

First, build your grip on the firearm like we discussed earlier in the book. **Spread, Torque, Press.**

Second, set your vision. You need to be able to see the sights move in recoil to know what effect the recoil management you are applying is having on the gun through your shot string. If you are narrow target focused on the front sight it's a lot like seeing through a small window. As the gun goes off and through its recoil, it will leave that window and then return without you being able to see where it went and what it did. Set your vision so that you see "everything". Don't focus on the target, don't focus on the sights. Set your plane of focus somewhere in the middle so that you notice the surroundings with your peripherals.

Lastly, fire your rounds and "notice" what the sights are doing in recoil. Are they going straight up, off to the left, off to the right, too high, nose dips down, etc? This is your indicator of what you need to do

here. As you shoot your strings, see the entire recoil process of the sights lifting (calling your shot) and returning (follow-through). You can think of it as one continuous sight picture, instead of a second and third after each shot.

CONCLUSION

Recoil management is not only about locking the gun so that sights lift and return in the same way. It's just as much about vision. See through your sights so that you can get feedback on what your sights are doing through recoil. See the lift so in the future you can call the shot. See the sights return so that you have good follow through.

START POSITION

Standing at the 3 m cone, facing down range, holding gun with sights on paster, gun fully loaded.

PROCEDURE

Shooter holds sights on target with trigger at the wall, then shoots a 2 or 3 round string only as fast as you can see the sights lift and return to the same index point, and feel how you are framing out the pistol.

Find what right feels and looks like, then repeat that for each paster building consistency.

DO

- Reset the sights and trigger as fast as possible.
- Frame the pistol out so the sights return the same spot.
- Shoot at a pace you can think and feel your way through it.

FEEL

- Your firing platform and spreading of the gun.
- Your support hand torquing forward.
- Your elbows wedging the gun forward for the sights to realign naturally.

SEE

- Equal height and equal light on top of your sights.
- The sights lift straight up to call your shot.
- The sights return onto the paster mirroring sight picture before.
- The return as lift in reverse.

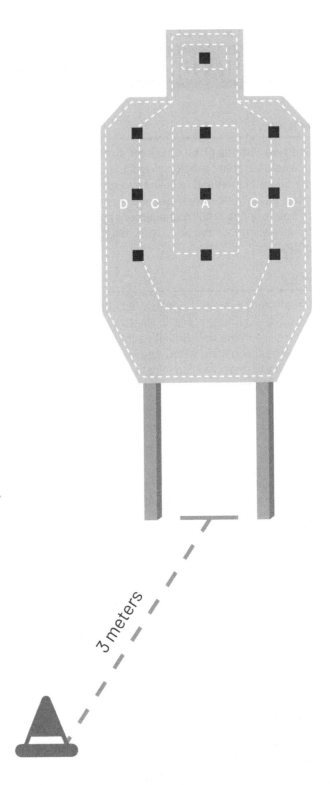

3 meters

VISION DRILLS

Near/Far Focus Drill

Task

Place the Far grid on the wall, assume a full presentation pistol stance with the corresponding Near grid in your hands. Shift your focus from far to near as fast as possible, maintaining crystal clear images on both the near and far grids. Complete as many iterations as possible, pushing into eye and concentration fatigue.

Purpose

Condition visual system to shift focal planes from far to near and back.

Focus

1. Crystal clear images for each box of each respective grid
2. Shifting focus between grids as fast as possible

1st Progression

Use grids Near1 and Far1 or Near2 and Far2. Begin with the upper left-hand box on the far grid and shift your focus as fast as possible to the upper left-hand box on the near grid. Repeat this process, moving from the left to the right for as many rows as possible until either eye or concentration fatigue results in slowed shifts or unclear images. Record your progress on the chart below by noting the row and column of the last image you were able to shift your focus.

D ate	F /C	D ate	F /C	D ate	F /C	D ate	F /C	D ate	F /C

2nd Progression

Use grids Near3 and Far3. Follow the same concept as the 1st Progression, but this time, work from the upper left box down the column and continue until the grids are complete or you've completed as many columns as possible. Record your progress on the chart below.

D ate	F /C	D ate	F /C	D ate	F /C	D ate	F /C	D ate	F /C

3rd Progression

Use grids Near4 and Far4. Follow the same concept as before, but this time, start with the numbers moving diagonally from left to right, then right to left. Finish by just seeing the letters starting at the top left and moving left to right, top to bottom. Record your progress on the chart below.

Date	F/C	Date	F/C	Date	F/C	Date	F/C	Date	F/C

S	L	A	C	K	S	I	G	H	T
S	Q	U	E	E	Z	E	S	E	E
T	H	R	O	U	G	H	T	H	E
R	E	C	O	I	L	T	R	I	G
G	E	R	R	E	S	E	T	S	E
C	O	N	D	S	I	G	H	T	P
I	C	T	U	R	E	S	C	A	N
G	R	I	P	S	T	A	N	C	E
F	O	C	A	L	P	L	A	N	E

Far1

C	A	L	M	C	O	O	L	C	O
L	L	E	C	T	E	D	D	O	T
H	E	W	O	R	K	S	I	G	H
T	S	L	A	C	K	S	Q	U	E
E	Z	E	B	A	N	G	F	A	S
T	H	A	N	D	S	Q	U	I	E
T	M	I	N	D	W	I	N	I	T
F	I	N	E	F	O	C	U	S	I
A	M	P	R	E	P	A	R	E	D

Far2

①	G	S	Q	O	I	N	U	E	❾
②	R	T	U	N	C	T	C	Y	❽
③	I	R	E	D	T	A	H	E	❼
④	P	I	E	S	U	C	P	S	❻
⑤	S	G	Z	I	R	M	O	F	❺
⑥	I	G	E	G	E	A	I	I	❹
⑦	G	E	S	H	S	G	N	R	❸
⑧	H	R	E	T	C	T	T	S	❷
⑨	T	S	C	P	A	O	S	T	❶

Far3

(1)	F	A	D	E	T	O	B	L	●1
A	(2)	C	K	◗	D	R	A	●2	W
S	I	(3)	G	H	T	S	●3	L	A
C	K	S	(4)	Q	U	●4	E	E	Z
E	◗	S	E	(5)	●5	E	T	H	R
O	U	G	H	●6	(6)	T	H	◗	E
R	E	C	●7	O	I	(7)	L	E	Y
E	S	●8	F	I	◗	S	(8)	T	S
C	●9	A	N	A	F	T	E	(9)	R

Far4

Near1

S	L	A	C	K	S	I	G	H	T
S	Q	U	E	E	Z	E	S	E	E
T	H	R	O	U	G	H	T	H	E
R	E	C	O	I	L	T	R	I	G
G	E	R	R	E	S	E	T	S	E
C	O	N	D	S	I	G	H	T	P
I	C	T	U	R	E	S	C	A	N
G	R	I	P	S	T	A	N	C	E
F	O	C	A	L	P	L	A	N	E

Near1

Near2

C	A	L	M	C	O	O	L	C	O
L	L	E	C	T	E	D	D	O	T
H	E	W	O	R	K	S	I	G	H
T	S	L	A	C	K	S	Q	U	E
E	Z	E	B	A	N	G	F	A	S
T	H	A	N	D	S	Q	U	I	E
T	M	I	N	D	W	I	N	I	T
F	I	N	E	F	O	C	U	S	I
A	M	P	R	E	P	A	R	E	D

Near2

Near3

(1)	G	S	Q	O	I	N	U	E	(9)
(2)	R	T	U	N	C	T	C	Y	(8)
(3)	I	R	E	D	T	A	H	E	(7)
(4)	P	I	E	S	U	C	P	S	(6)
(5)	S	G	Z	I	R	M	O	F	(5)
(6)	I	G	E	G	E	A	I	I	(4)
(7)	G	E	S	H	S	G	N	R	(3)
(8)	H	R	E	T	C	T	T	S	(2)
(9)	T	S	C	P	A	O	S	T	(1)

Near3

Near4

(1)	F	A	D	E	T	O	B	L	(1)
A	(2)	C	K	[icon]	D	R	A	(2)	W
S	I	(3)	G	H	T	S	(3)	L	A
C	K	S	(4)	Q	U	(4)	E	E	Z
E	[icon]	S	E	(5)	(5)	E	T	H	R
O	U	G	H	(6)	(6)	T	H	[icon]	E
R	E	C	(7)	O	I	(7)	L	E	Y
E	S	(8)	F	I	[icon]	S	(8)	T	S
C	(9)	A	N	A	F	T	E	(9)	R

Near4

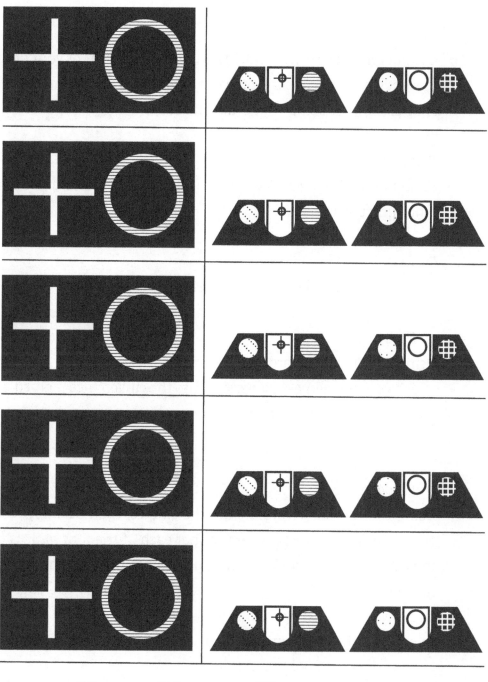

Binocular Vision Drill

Task

Cut out one of the cards below. Hold the card in front of your nose and move it closer or further from your face until you can merge the two shapes together using your binocular focus.

Purpose

Condition both halves of your binocular visual system to work more efficiently together.

Focus

    1.   Creating and maintaining the merged shapes

1st Progression

Using the Crosshair card, find the precise distance from your nose at which you can merge the plus sign into the circle. Once merged, slowly move the card further from your face while maintaining the merged image.

2nd Progression

Using the Crosshair card, merge the shapes, then attempt to move the circle around the plus sign so that each of the four ends is touching the edge of the circle. Then, while maintaining the merged image, move each individual end of the plus sign to touch the edge of the circle. Notice which eye seems to be doing most of the work. Then try to use the other eye to move the plus sign to touch the circle.

3rd Progression

Using either card, merge the shapes together and move your head and hands, holding the card to the left and right in one motion as if your upper body is a turret. Next, repeat the same process while moving up and down, then diagonally. Focus on keeping the merged image intact throughout the movements.

4th Progression

Using either card, merge the shapes together and move only the card and your eyes, keeping your head still. Focus on keeping the image merged throughout the movement. Start by moving the card left and right, then up and down, then diagonally, then in random patterns.

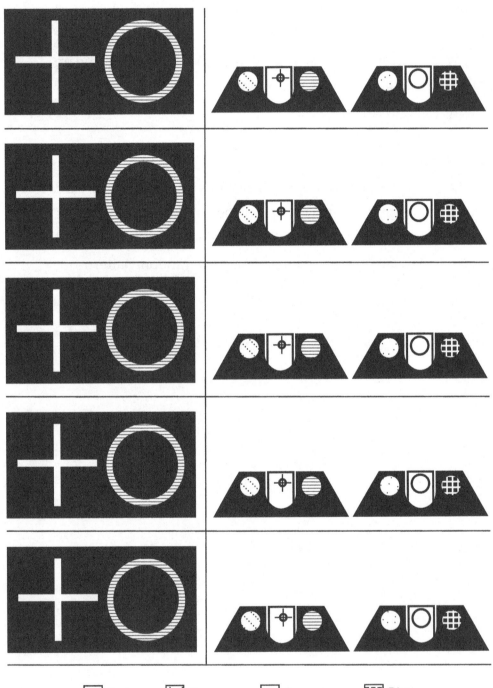

 Red   Green   Orange   Blue

ACKNOWLEDGMENTS

When I started writing this book, I knew it would be hard. What I didn't know is how many people would help with it. Originally, I started thinking about it while I was still in the military during a deployment in 2016. Needless to say, it has changed and morphed over time to meet the needs of who I thought would be reading it. In 2018, I started to take it seriously and worked on it. After bouncing ideas off of former students and people I trained with, I started over. After sharing it with people like Dave Rhoden, I started over again. The publisher, editing team, and Sarafina were a godsend. Y'all made it a real book.

After getting out of the military, I truly learned the importance of family. To my wife and daughter, thank you for giving me a purpose to be a better man every day. House BAER.

Mom: You've always set the example of an incredible woman. If you weren't my mother, I wouldn't have kept going.

Dad: I wouldn't have lived up to my potential if you hadn't told me, "You can do anything," while growing up. You never put a limit on Kevin's and my potential.

Brosef Kevin: Dude, I wrote a book. Crazy right? You're a good man, and thank you for being my brother.

Joe Neill: For countless days on the range pushing each other to be better, analyzing what others wouldn't think of, and in some cases maybe shouldn't. I appreciate you.

Seth Haselhuhn: Special thanks for all the hours sitting in your office arguing about the best ways to teach shooting. Also, for playing such a big part in making all of us better at our jobs. I am a product of your mentorship and friendship.

Those who set the example in this industry, some I've had the privilege of meeting, and others I haven't: Kyle Lamb, JJ Racaza, Ron Avery, and a host of others.

Garett Schwindel, Ian Strimbeck, and Mike Jones: Thank you for your support and friendship. BAER Solutions wouldn't be here without you guys and a host of others.

To my teammates at BAER Solutions, Steve, Paul, and Mitch: "Yeah, you right."

To all the men of Fifth Special Forces Group and the Special Forces Regiment. I hope we represent you well.

To all the law enforcement officers who have shared their knowledge, and especially the guys and gals out in Kansas.

To all the people who have come to a class and supported BAER Solutions: You da best. Thank you.

Made in the USA
Middletown, DE
11 February 2024

49503465R00104